PHILIP'S

STRE[ET]

York

First published 2002 by

Philip's, a division of
Octopus Publishing Group Ltd
2–4 Heron Quays
London E14 4JP

First edition 2002
First impression 2002

ISBN 0 540 08331 3
© Philip's 2002

 Ordnance Survey®

This product includes mapping data licensed
from Ordnance Survey®, with the
permission of the Controller of Her Majesty's
Stationery Office.© Crown copyright 2002.
All rights reserved.
Licence number 100011710

The bus route maps on page 74 and the
inside back cover are reproduced with the
permission of First, in York

Photographs on pages VI and VII:
James Hughes

Printed and bound in Spain
by Cayfosa-Quebecor.

Contents

MIKE DUGHER

FLOOD DEFENCE

DARLINGTON

Key to map symbols

Roads

(12)	**Motorway** with junction number
A42	**Primary route** – dual/single carriageway
A42	**A road** – dual/single carriageway
B1289	**B road** – dual/single carriageway
	Through-route – dual/single carriageway
	Minor road – dual/single carriageway
	Rural track, private road or narrow road in urban area
	Path, bridleway, byway open to all traffic, road used as a public path
	Road under construction
	Pedestrianised area
	Gate or obstruction to traffic restrictions may not apply at all times or to all vehicles
P P&R	**Parking, Park and Ride**

Railways

	Railway
	Miniature railway
⇄ 🚂	**Railway station, private railway station**

Emergency services

◆ ◆	**Ambulance station, coastguard station**
◆ ◆	**Fire station, police station**
H ✚	**Hospital, Accident and Emergency entrance to hospital**

General features

✚ PO	**Place of worship, Post Office**
𝒊	**Information centre** (open all year)
	Bus, coach station
	Important buildings, schools, colleges, universities and hospitals
	Woods, built-up area
Tumulus FORT	**Non-Roman antiquity, Roman antiquity**

Leisure facilities

⛺ 🚐	**Camping site, caravan site**
▶ ✕	**Golf course, picnic site**

Boundaries

• • • • • • • •	**Postcode boundaries**
— • — • —	**County and unitary authority boundaries**

Water features

River Ouse	**Tidal water, water name**
	Non-tidal water – lake, river, canal or stream
‹		**Lock, weir**

Scales

Green pages: 2¼ inches to 1 mile 1:28160

0   ¼ mile   ½ mile   ¾ mile   1 mi

0   250m   500m   750m   1km

Blue pages: 4½ inches to 1 mile 1:14080

0   220 yds   ¼ mile   660 yds   ½ m

0   125m   250m   375m   ½ km

Red pages: 7 inches to 1 mile 1:9051

0   110 yds   220 yds   330 yds   ¼ mile

0   125m   250m   375m   ½km

123	**Adjoining page indicators** The colour of the arrow and the band indicates the scale of the adjoining page (see above)

Abbreviations

Acad	Academy		Mkt	Market
Allot Gdns	Allotments		Meml	Memorial
Cemy	Cemetery		Mon	Monument
C Ctr	Civic Centre		Mus	Museum
CH	Club House		Obsy	Observatory
Coll	College		Pal	Royal Palace
Crem	Crematorium		PH	Public House
Ent	Enterprise		Recn Gd	Recreation Ground
Ex H	Exhibition Hall		Resr	Reservoir
Ind Est	Industrial Estate		Ret Pk	Retail Park
IRB Sta	Inshore Rescue Boat Station		Sch	School
Inst	Institute		Sh Ctr	Shopping Centre
Ct	Law Court		TH	Town Hall/House
L Ctr	Leisure Centre		Trad Est	Trading Estate
LC	Level Crossing		Univ	University
Liby	Library		Wks	Works
			YH	Youth Hostel

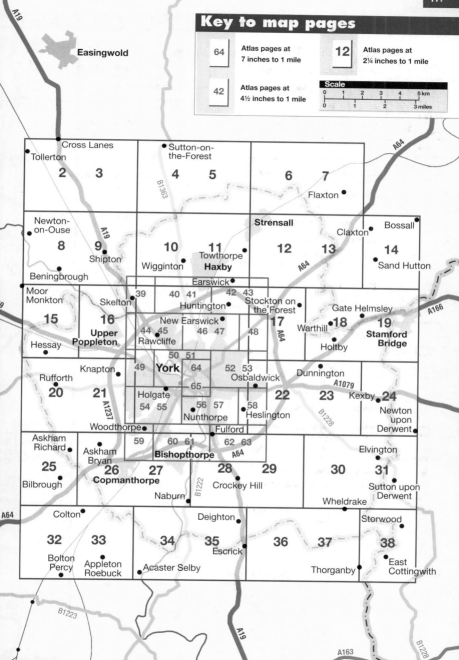

III

Key to map pages

64	Atlas pages at 7 inches to 1 mile
12	Atlas pages at 2¼ inches to 1 mile
42	Atlas pages at 4½ inches to 1 mile

Scale
0 1 2 3 4 5 km
0 1 2 3 miles

Easingwold

A19

A64

Cross Lanes
Tollerton
2 **3**

Sutton-on-the-Forest
4 **5**

6 **7**
Flaxton

B1363

Newton-on-Ouse
8 **9**
Shipton

10 Towthorpe
11
Wigginton **Haxby**

Strensall
12 **13**
Claxton Bossall

14
Sand Hutton

Beningbrough
Earswick

Moor Monkton
Skelton
15 **16**
Upper Poppleton
Hessay

39
40 41 42 43
Huntington
New Earswick
44 45 46 47
Rawcliffe 48

Stockton on the Forest
17
Warthill **18** **19**
Gate Helmsley **Stamford Bridge**
Holtby

A64

A166

Knapton
Rufforth
20 **21**
A1237

50 51
49 **York** 64
65
Holgate
54 55

52 53
Osbaldwick
56 57
Nunthorpe 58 Heslington
Woodthorpe Fulford

Dunnington
22 **23** Kexby **24**
Newton upon Derwent
A1079
B1228

Askham Richard
25 Askham Bryan **26 Copmanthorpe**
Bilbrough

59
60 61
62 63
Bishopthorpe A64
Naburn B1222

27 **28** **29**
Crockey Hill

Elvington
30 **31**
Sutton upon Derwent
Wheldrake

Colton
32 **33**
Bolton Percy Appleton Roebuck

34 **35**
Acaster Selby Escrick
Deighton

36 **37**
Thorganby

Storwood
38
East Cottingwith

B1223

A19
A163
B1228
A64
59

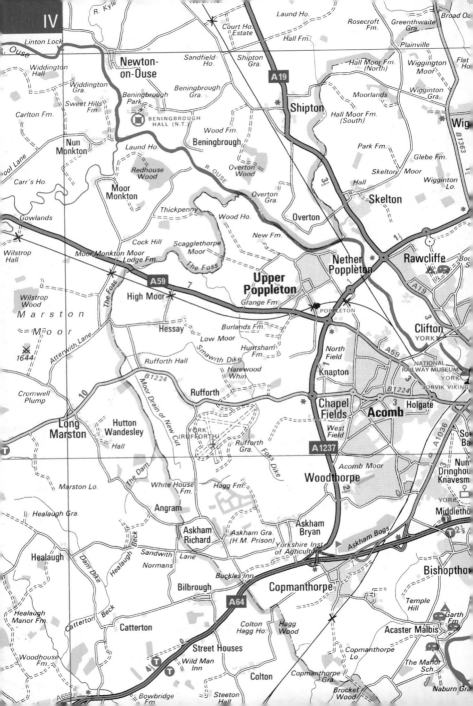

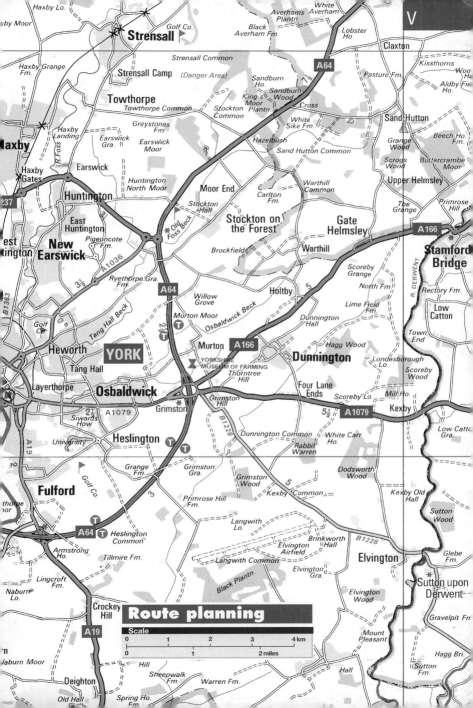

Sights of York

One star * indicates highly recommended sights

Two stars ** indicate sights of exceptional interest

City defences

Bar Walls * *Around central York* (also known as the City Walls) There have been defensive walls surrounding York since Roman times. The walls have since been demolished in places and added to, but some Roman masonry can be found in their foundations. They are named 'Bar Walls' after their gates, or bars, used for entry to and defence of the city. Micklegate bar is the largest of the remaining gatehouses.

Bootham Bar *High Petergate* Stands on the site of former Roman gateway and has some of earliest medieval stonework on the walls. 64 B3

Clifford's Tower (EH) * *Tower Street* Built around 1250 at the same time as the castle. The Lancastrian leader Roger de Clifford was hanged here in 1322 for opposing Edward II. 65 B1

Fishergate Postern Tower *Piccadilly* Built between 1504 and 1507. 65 C1

Micklegate Bar * *Micklegate* The 12th-century royal gateway to York, the portcullis was added in 14th century. The site where traitors' heads were displayed and civic ceremonies took place. 65 A1

Monk Bar * *Goodramgate* Built in 14th century, still with operational portcullis. Houses Richard III museum. 64 C3

Multangular Tower *Museum Gardens* Built as part of Roman defences, probably around 210, only part of the remaining tower is Roman. 64 A3

The Red Tower *Navigation Road* Built in 15th century and used as a stable in 18th century. The only brick tower. 52 A1

Robin Hood Tower *Lord Mayors Walk* Built by the Victorians on the site of previous towers in the style of a medieval tower. 64 B3

St Mary's Tower *Bootham* Built 14th century and rebuilt after the Civil War. 64 A3

Victoria Bar *Victoria Street* Opened 1838 in response to population growth. 65 B1

Walmgate Bar Rectangular two-storey gatehouse. The only bar to still have both the portcullis and barbican and the wooden doors. 57 A4

York Castle * *Tower Street* Original castle built in 1068 by William the Conqueror but rebuilt in 13th century. After the Civil War it became a prison; some prison buildings remain. 65 C1

Historic buildings

Bedern Hall *Bedern* 14th-century former refectory of the Vicars Choral, now used as a function room. Not open. 64 C3

Black Swan public house *Peasholme Green* 16–17th century half-timbered merchant's house, now a pub. ☎01904 686911 65 C2

Grand Assembly Rooms *Blake Street* Historic building, currently leased as a restaurant. Available to view during restaurant opening hours. ☎01904 637254 64 B3

The Guildhall *St Helens Square* Replica of the 15th-century building, the original was destroyed by fire in an air raid in 1942. ☎01904 551010 65 B2

King's Manor * *Exhibition Square* Historic building owned by the University of York. 16th-century seat of the Council of the North. 64 B3

Mansion House *St Helens Square* Georgian house, home to the city's Lord Mayors since the 18th century. Not open. 65 B2

Merchant Adventurers' Hall * *Fossgate* Built 1350s. Possibly Europe's finest medieval guildhall. ☎01904 654818 65 C2

Merchant Taylors' Hall *Aldwark* 14th-century craft guildhall. ☎01904 624889 64 C3

Roman Bath Public House *St Sampsons Square* Pub with Roman bath in basement discovered during renovation. Can be viewed from a suspended walkway. ☎01904 620455 65 B2

St Anthony's Hall *Peasholme Green* Partly 15th century. Now the Borthwick Institute of Historical Research at the University of York. Open to the public. ☎01904 642315 65 C2

St William's College *College Street* Timbered 15th century building, originally college for Minster Chantry priests. Medieval halls open to view. Now home to York Minster Information & Conference Centre and a restaurant. 64 B3

Houses

Barley Hall *Coffee Yard* Restored medieval merchant's house, home to Alderman Snawsell. ☎01904 610275 64 B3

▲ *Low Petergate*

Beningbrough Hall and Gardens (NT) * *Beningbrough* Baroque house. Contains portraits loaned by the National Portrait Gallery. Gardens and parkland. ☎01904 470666 8 A2

Bishopthorpe Palace *Bishopthorpe Road* Official home of Archbishop of York in 9 acres of grounds. Only open for pre-booked groups. ☎01904 707021 61 A1

Brockfield Hall *Warthill* Georgian country house. Limited opening throughout August, appointment only all other times. ☎01904 489298 18 A3

Fairfax House *Castlegate* 18th-century town house. ☎01904 655543 65 B2

Sutton Park * *Sutton-on-the-Forest* Early Georgian house built 1730. Gardens overlook spacious parkland. ☎01347 810249 4 B4

Treasurer's House NT * *Minster Yard* 17th-18th century town house. ☎01904 624247 64 B3

▼ *York Minster* seen from the city wall near Monk Bar

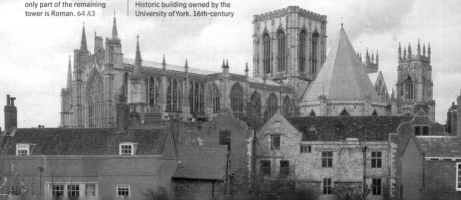

Gardens and parks

Museum Gardens ★ *Museum Street* Yorkshire Museum set in 10 acres of botanical gardens. ☎01904 551800 64 A3

War Memorial Gardens *Leeman Road* Parkland and memorial 65 A2

Rowntree Park *Terry Avenue* 20 acres of parkland on the River Ouse. 56 B3

West Bank Park *Acomb* Park and formal gardens. 55 A4

Churches

York Minster ★★ *Deangate* Largest medieval cathedral in Northern Europe, it took over 250 years to build. Octagonal chapter house. Undercroft treasury and crypt with Roman, Saxon and Norman remains. Crypt contains parts of the original Norman cathedral and the coffin of St William. ☎01904 557216 64 B3

All Saints ★ *North Street* Medieval stained glass windows. 65 B2

All Saints *Pavement* Tower with octagonal lantern. 65 B2

Holy Trinity ★ *Goodramgate* In quiet churchyard. 15th-century stained glass, box pews. 64 B3

Holy Trinity *Micklegate* Medieval church containing the city's stocks. 65 A2

St Cuthberts *Peasholme Green* Oldest church in York after the Minster. The walls include some Roman stone. 64 C3

St Denys *Walmgate* Old church with Norman porch and rare glass. 64 C3

St Helens *St Helen's Square* York's civic church with 15th-century glass. 65 B2

St Mary's Abbey *Museum Gardens* The 11th-century abbey was replaced by a new Gothic church in the 13th century. The impressive ruins of the church can be seen in the Museum Gardens. 64 A3

St Marys *Bishophill Junior* Saxon tower. Temple Moore altar-piece. 65 A1

St Michael-le-Belfry *Minster Yard* Dates back to 1570, contains baptism register for Guy Fawkes. 65 B2

St Martin-le-Grand ★ *Coney Street* Badly bombed 15th-century church, restored 1960s. Shrine to dead of both world wars. 65 B2

St Olaves *Marygate* Present church is 14th century with 18th-century restoration. 64 A3

Museums and galleries

The Bar Convent Museum *Blossom Street* Early history of Christianity in the north of England. ☎01904 643238 65 A1

Impressions Gallery *Castlegate* Contemporary photographic and new media installation work by British and international artists. Located in Georgian townhouse.

Jorvik – The Viking City ★★ *Coppergate* Reconstruction and artefacts from the Viking village Jorvik based on archaeological finds in York. ☎ 01904 643211 65 B2

Micklegate Bar Museum *On the Bar Walls* History of York. ☎01904 634436 65 A1

National Railway Museum ★★ *Leeman Road* Largest railway museum in the world. Collection includes Royal trains, record breaking Mallard locomotive and a replica of Stephenson's Rocket. ☎01904 621261 50 C1

Regimental Museum *Tower Street* History of two of Yorkshire's famous regiments, the Royal Dragoon Guards, and the Prince of Wales's Own Regiment of Yorkshire. ☎01904 662790 65 B2

Richard III Museum *Monkbar Gatehouse* Exhibition tells the story of Richard III, (King of England 1483-85). ☎01904 634191 64 C3

York Castle Museum *The Castle, off Tower Street.* Famous for its collections of costume, textiles, military and social history. ☎01904 653611 65 C1

York City Art Gallery ★ *Exhibition Square* 600 years of painting housed in 19th-century Italian Renaissance-style building. ☎01904 551861 64 B3

York Dungeon *Clifford Street* Museum of horror. ☎01904 632599 65 B2

▼ St William's College

Yorkshire Air Museum ★ *Elvington* Preserved wartime airfield with aircraft, including only complete Halifax in the world. ☎01904 608595 30 B4

Yorkshire Museum ★ *Museum Gardens* Covers 1000 years of Yorkshire's heritage. ☎01904 551800 64 A3

Yorkshire Museum of Farming *Murton Lane* Archives, exhibits and farm vehicle displays. ☎01904 489966 22 C4

Activities

The Archaeological Resource Centre (ARC) ★ *St Saviours Church, St Saviourgate* Linked to the Jorvik Viking Centre. Handle and examine archaeological finds with trained archaeologist staff. ☎01904 643211 65 C2

Barbican Centre *Barbican Road* Leisure centre and auditorium. ☎01904 656688 (box office), 01904 630266 (sports), 01904 670977 (recorded info) 65 C1

Grand Opera House *Cumberland Street* Venue for a variety of events including shows, musicals, ballets etc. ☎01904 671818 65 B2

National Centre for Early Music *St Margaret's Church, Walmgate* Centre for the study of early music. Venue for concerts, drama performances, conferences and workshops. ☎01904 632220 65 C2

Theatre Royal *St Leonard's Place* Much of present building dates from 19th century although the theatre dates back to 1744. ☎01904 623568 64 B3

Yorvik Brass Rubbing Centre *Skeldergate* Housed in almshouse built 1899.

Collection of Medieval and Tudor brass facsimiles available for visitors to make rubbings. ☎01904 611570 65 B1

York Brewery Tour *Toft Green, Micklegate* Independent brewery, beer is brewed using traditional methods. Daily guided tours around the brewery. ☎01904 621162 65 A2

York Model Railway *Tea Room Square, York Station* 323 metres of Hornby track with up to 14 trains running daily. ☎01904 630169 65 A2

Other sights

Lendal Tower The tower at the eastern end of Lendal Bridge originally served as a defence but was adapted to a waterworks in 17th century. 65 A2

The Shambles ★ One of the best preserved medieval streets in Europe. Some buildings date back to 1350. 65 B2

Goodramgate Lady Row dates from the 14th century. Now houses small collection of shops. 64 B3

Grape Lane One of the oldest streets in the city. 64 B3

Newgate Market *Off Parliament Street* Fresh produce market open daily 8am–5pm. ☎01904 551355 65 B2

University of York *Heslington* Established in 1963. The university owns a number of important and historic buildings in the city. (See King's Manor) ☎01904 430000 58 A3

York Racecourse *Knavesmire* Top class horse racing from May to October. ☎01904 620911 60 C4

Information

York Tourist Office *Exhibition Square* ☎01904 621756 64 B3

York Police Station *Fulford Road* ☎01904 631321 56 C2

York District Hospital (Accident & Emergency) *Wigginton Road* ☎01904 631313 64 B4

Carpark Helpline ☎01904 632735

Bus Enquiries ☎01904 551400

National Rail Enquiries ☎08457 484950

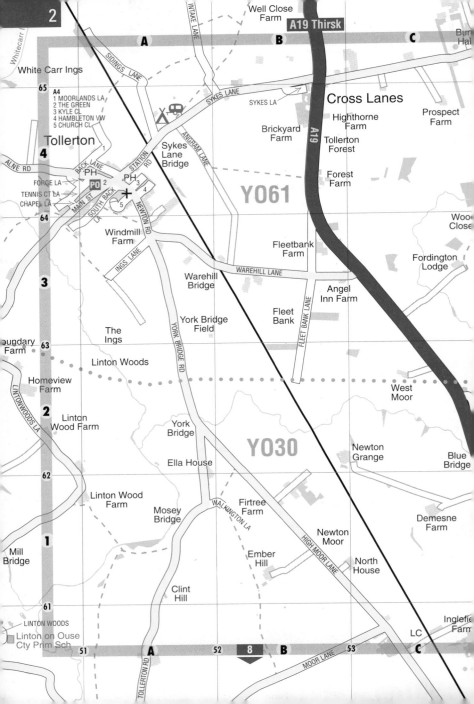

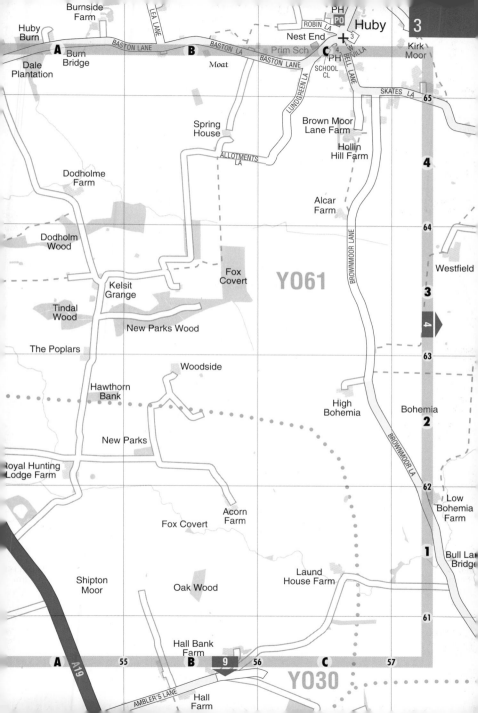

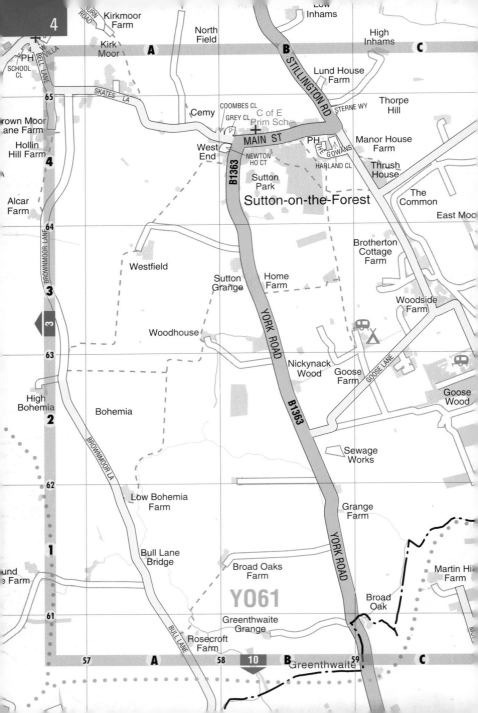

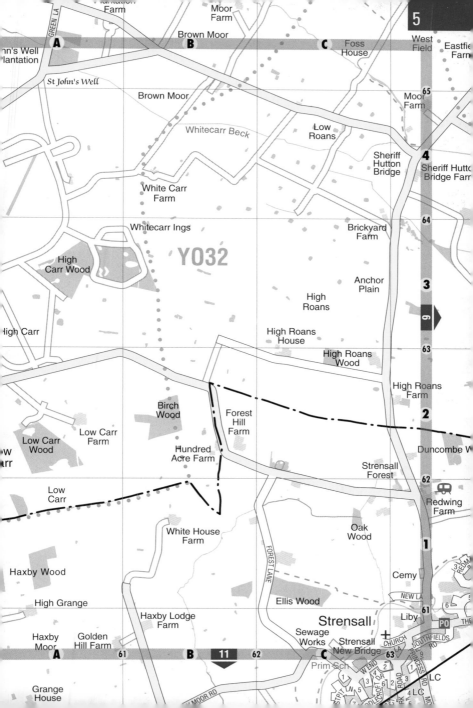

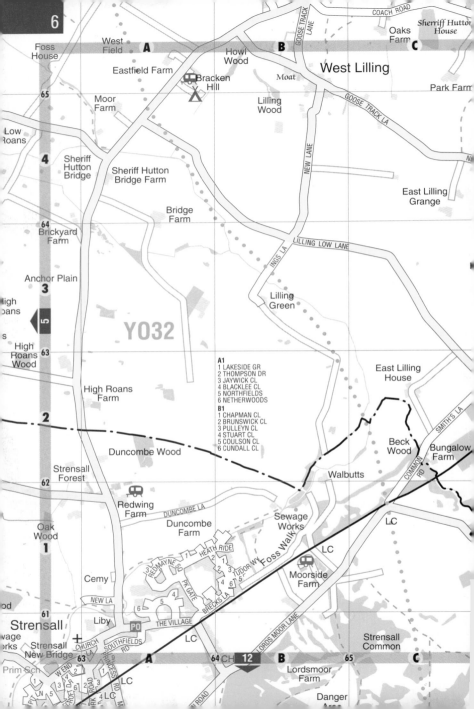

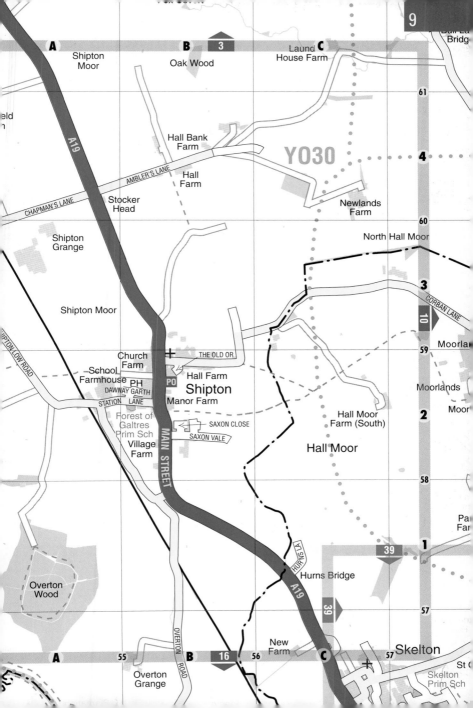

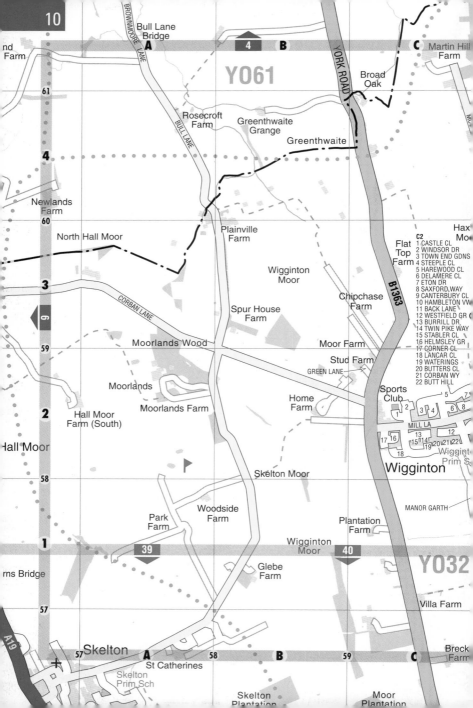

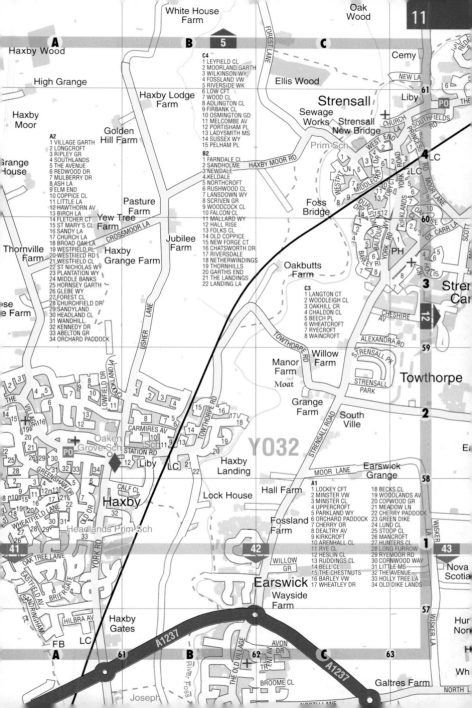

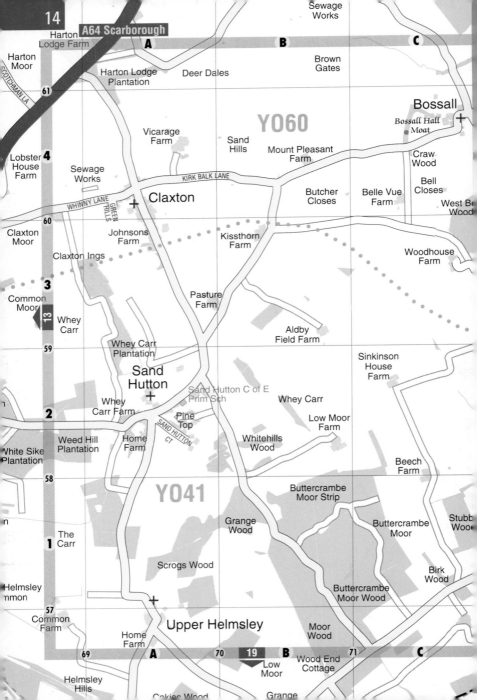

A64 Scarborough

Sewage Works

Harton Lodge Farm

A

B

C

Harton Moor

Harton Lodge Plantation

Deer Dales

Brown Gates

SCOTCHMAN LA

61

Bossall

YO60

Bossall Hall Moat

Vicarage Farm

Sand Hills

Mount Pleasant Farm

Craw Wood

Lobster House Farm

4

Sewage Works

KIRK BALK LANE

Butcher Closes

Belle Vue Farm

Bell Closes

WHINNY LANE

Claxton

GREEN HILLS

West B Wood

60

Claxton Moor

Johnsons Farm

Kissthorn Farm

Woodhouse Farm

Claxton Ings

Common Moor

3

13

Pasture Farm

Whey Carr

Aldby Field Farm

Whey Carr Plantation

59

Sinkinson House Farm

Sand Hutton

Sand Hutton C of E Prim Sch

Whey Carr

2

Whey Carr Farm

SAND HUTTON CT

Pine Top

Low Moor Farm

White Sike Plantation

Weed Hill Plantation

Home Farm

Whitehills Wood

Beech Farm

58

YO41

Buttercrambe Moor Strip

Grange Wood

Buttercrambe Moor

Stubb Woo

1

The Carr

Scrogs Wood

Buttercrambe Moor Wood

Birk Wood

Helmsley nmon

57

Common Farm

Home Farm

Upper Helmsley

Moor Wood

69

70

19

71

A

B

Low Moor

Wood End Cottage

C

Helmsley Hills

Grange

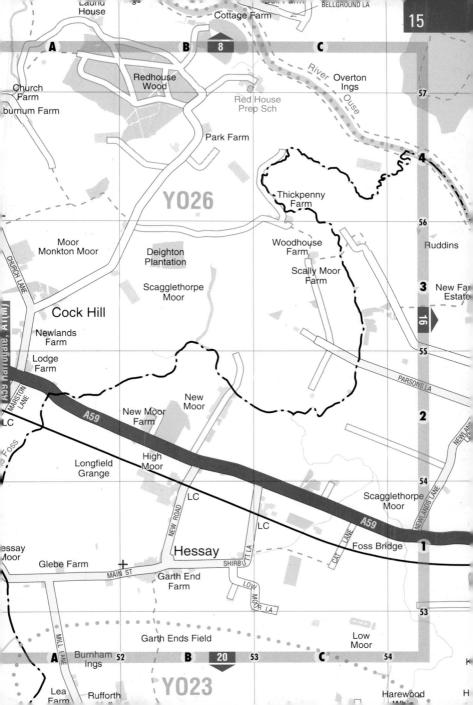

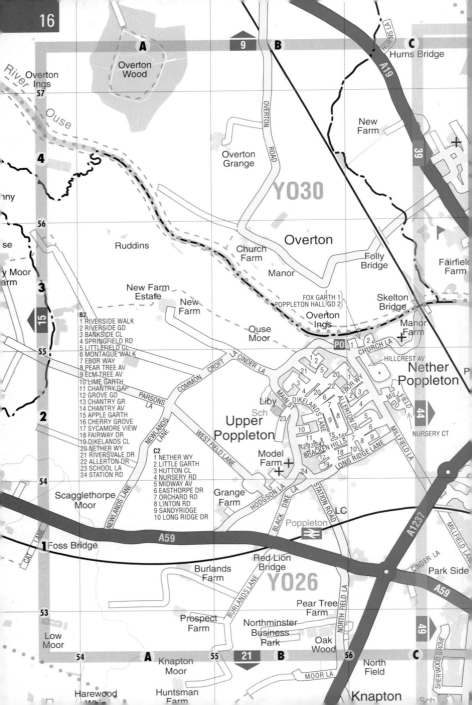

River Ouse

Overton Ings
57

Overton Wood

A 9 B

Hurns Bridge C

A19 39

New Farm

4

Overton Grange

OVERTON ROAD

YO30

56

Ruddins

Overton

Church Farm

Manor

Folly Bridge

Fairfield Farm

3

New Farm Estate

New Farm

15

B2
1 RIVERSIDE WALK
2 RIVERSIDE GD
3 BANKSIDE CL
4 SPRINGFIELD RD
5 LITTLEFIELD CL
6 MONTAGUE WALK
7 EBOR WAY
8 PEAR TREE AV
9 ELM TREE AV
10 LIME GARTH
11 CHANTRY GAP
12 GROVE GD
13 CHANTRY GR
14 CHANTRY AV
15 APPLE GARTH
16 CHERRY GROVE
17 SYCAMORE VIEW
18 FAIRWAY DR
19 DIKELANDS CL
20 NETHER WY
21 RIVERSVALE DR
22 ALLERTON DR
23 SCHOOL LA
24 STATION RD

55

FOX GARTH 1
POPPLETON HALL GD 2

Overton Ings

Skelton Bridge

Manor Farm

PO

CHURCH LA

HILLCREST AV

Nether Poppleton

2

COMMON CROFT LA

CINDER LA

PARSONS LA

NEWLANDS LANE

Liby Sch

MAIN ST

DIKELANDS LANE

EBOR WY

ALLERTON DR

MILL FIELD GD

NURSERY CT

44

54

Upper Poppleton

WEST FIELD LANE

BRACKEN HILLS

LONG RIDGE LANE

MILL FIELD LA

C2
1 NETHER WY
2 LITTLE GARTH
3 HUTTON CL
4 NURSERY RD
5 MIDWAY AV
6 EASTHORPE DR
7 ORCHARD RD
8 LINTON RD
9 SANDYRIDGE
10 LONG RIDGE DR

Model Farm

Grange Farm

HODGSON LA

BLACK DIKE LA

STATION ROAD

LC

Poppleton

A1237

MILL FIELD LA

Scagglethorpe Moor

NEWLANDS LANE

CAT LANE

Foss Bridge

A59

Red Lion Bridge

YO26

Park Side

A59

53

Low Moor

Burlands Farm

Prospect Farm

BURLANDS LANE

Northminster Business Park

Oak Wood

NORTH FIELD LA

CINDER LA

49

SHERWOOD GROVE

54

A

Knapton Moor

55

21

B

56

C

North Field

MOOR LA

Harewood Whin

Huntsman Farm

Knapton

Sch

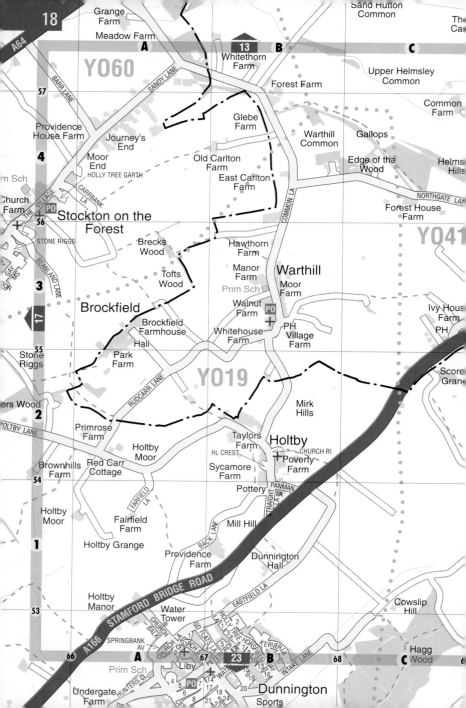

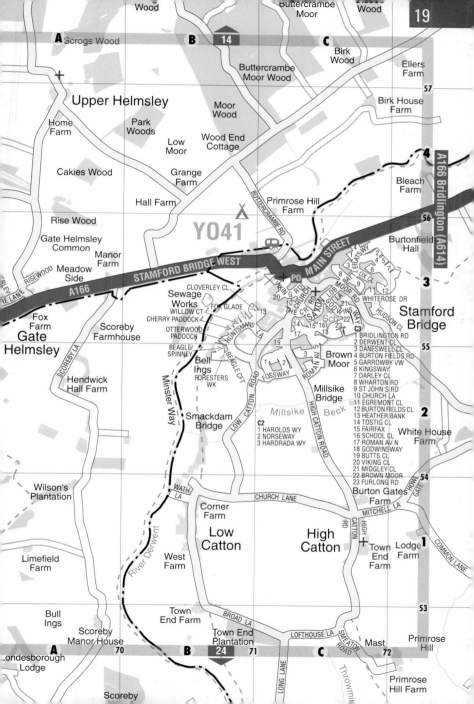

A Scrogs Wood **B** 14 **C**

Wood

Buttercrambe Moor

Wood

Birk Wood

Ellers Farm

57

Upper Helmsley

Buttercrambe Moor Wood

Moor Wood

Birk House Farm

Home Farm

Park Woods

Low Moor

Wood End Cottage

Bleach Farm

4 A166 Bridlington (A614)

Cakies Wood

Grange Farm

Primrose Hill Farm

56

Hall Farm

BUTTERCRAMBE RD

Burtonfield Hall

Rise Wood

YO41

MAIN STREET

3

Gate Helmsley Common

Manor Farm

STAMFORD BRIDGE WEST

EAST WY

OX CL

Whiterose Dr

Stamford Bridge

Meadow Side

A166

RISEWOOD

Fox Farm

Gate Helmsley

Scoreby Farmhouse

CLOVERLEY CL.

Sewage Works

FOX GLADE

WILLOW CT

CHERRY PADDOCK

OTTERWOOD PADDOCK

BEAGLE SPINNEY

Bell Ings

FORESTERS WK

VIKING RD

THE CR

SAXON

Sch

MOOR RD

GODWIN WY

HUDSON CL

C3

1 BRIDLINGTON RD
2 DERWENT CL
3 DANESWELL CL
4 BURTON FIELDS RD
5 GARROWBY VW
6 KINGSWAY
7 DARLEY CL
8 WHARTON RD
9 ST JOHN'S RD
10 CHURCH LA
11 EGREMONT CL
12 BURTON FIELDS CL
13 HEATHER BANK
14 TOSTIG CL
15 FAIRFAX
16 SCHOOL CL
17 ROMAN AV N
18 GODWINSWAY
19 BUTTS CL
20 VIKING CL
21 MIDGLEY CL
22 BROWN MOOR
23 FURLONG RD

55

Brown Moor

Hendwick Hall Farm

SCOREBY LA

Minster Way

HUNTSMANS LA

BEAGLE CFT

LOW CATTON ROAD

FOSSWAY

ROMAN AV

Millsike Bridge

Millsike Beck

High Catton Road

White House Farm

2

Smackdam Bridge

C2
1 HAROLDS WY
2 NORSEWAY
3 HARDRADA WY

54

Wilson's Plantation

WATH LA

Corner Farm

CHURCH LANE

Burton Gates Farm

MITCHELL LA

HORN GATE

Limefield Farm

Low Catton

High Catton

CATTON RD

HIGH

Lodge Farm

COMMON LANE

1

West Farm

Town End Farm

53

Bull Ings

Town End Farm

BROAD LA

River Derwent

Scoreby Manor House

Town End Plantation

LOFTHOUSE LA

SMEATON ROAD

Mast

Primrose Hill

ondesborough Lodge

A 70 **B** 24 71 **C** 72

LONG LANE

Throwmi

Primrose Hill Farm

Scoreby

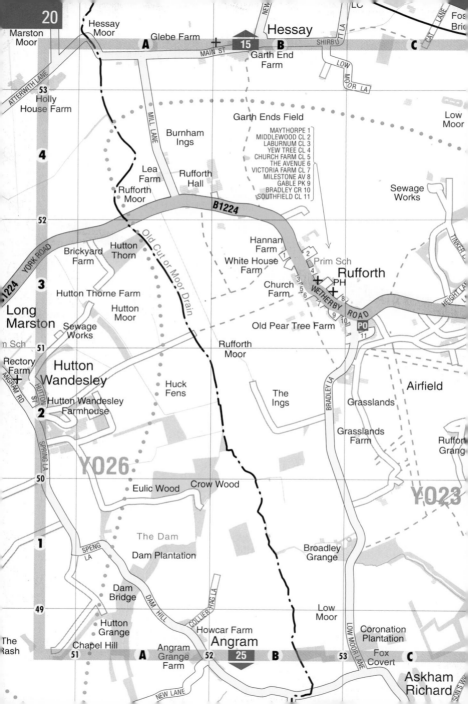

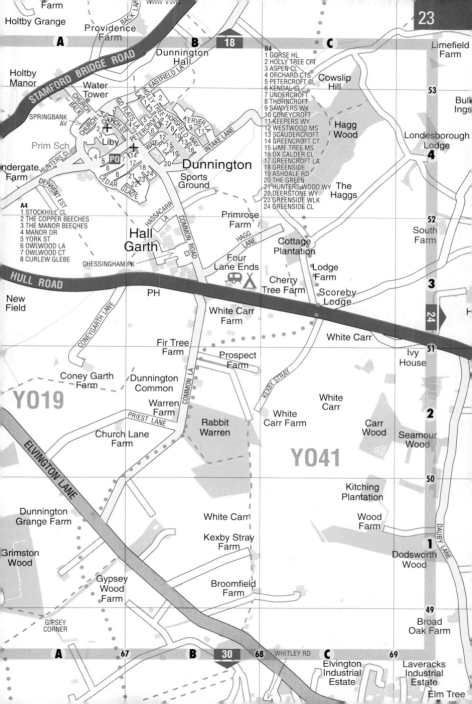

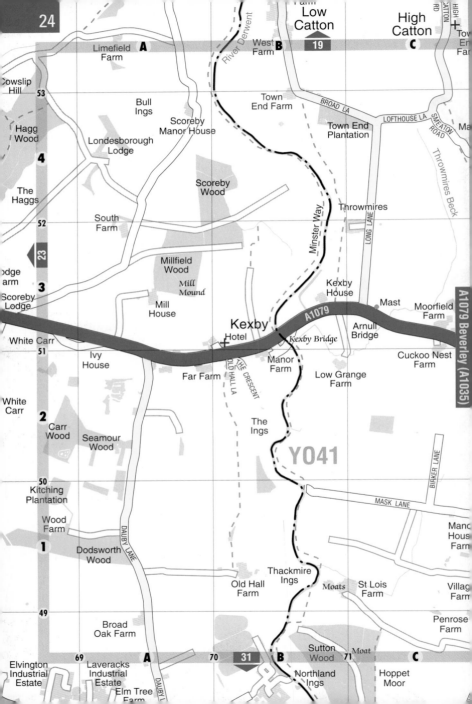

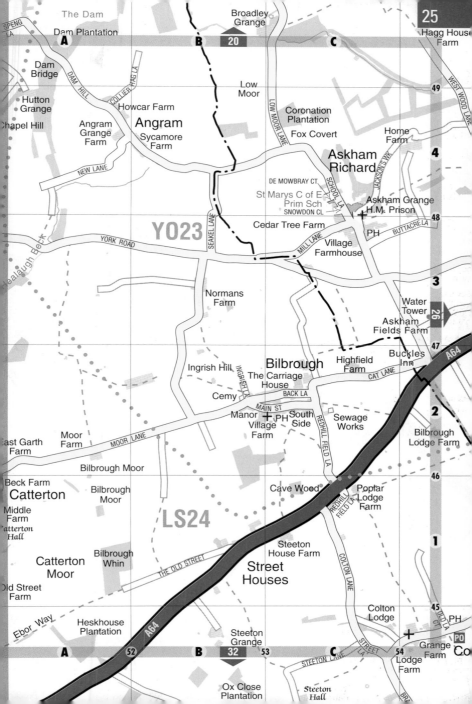

YO23

Hagg House Farm

A **21** B C

High Moor

49

Acomb Moor

Eastfield Farm

59

WEST WOOD LANE

NORTH FIELD LANE

ASKHAM BRYAN LANE

A1237

Askham Richard

4

Home Farm

CHURCH CL

Main St

Askham Bryan

ST NICHOLAS CFT PH

Askham Grange H.M. Prison

48

PH BUTTACRE LA

Village Farmhouse

3

JACKSON'S WK

SCHOOL LA

CHAPEL LANE

ASKHAM FIELDS LA

Sewage Works

MILL LA

ASKHAM FIELDS

Cotton End CH

A64

Water Tower

Askham Fields Farm

25

47

Buckles Inn

Highfield Farm

CAT LANE

A64

Eastbarrow Farm

Askham Bryan Coll

PIKE HILL MT

COLLEGE RD

MANOR HEATH

HORSEMAN LA

Copmanthorpe

TOP LANE

FLAXMAN

C2
1 MANOR FARM CL
2 CHURCH ST
3 REYGATE GR
4 MALBYS GR
5 VICARS CL
6 DEACONS CT
7 BELLMANS CFT
8 FAIRFAX CFT
9 BEADLE GARTH
10 VAVASOUR CT
11 WILSTROP FARM RD
12 HOMEFIELD CL
13 PADDOCK CL
14 BARNFIELD WY
15 HOBSON CL
16 NALTON CL
17 LEADLEY CFT
18 SCHOOL LA

Sewage Works

2

Bilbrough Lodge Farm

PRESTHILL FIELD LA

46

Poplar Lodge Farm

COLTON LANE

Colton Haggs Farm

Hagg Wood

LOW WESTFIELD ROAD

C3
1 THE LINK
2 ST NICHOLAS CR
3 ST NICHOLAS RD
4 ST NICHOLAS CL
5 LARKFIELD CL
6 LYNWOOD VW
7 RUTLAND CL
8 HORSEMAN DR
9 LYNWOOD AV
10 HORSEMAN CL
11 HORSEMAN AV
12 MILLERS CFT
13 WEAVERS CL
14 COOPERS DR
15 DRAPERS CFT
16 BARBERS DR
17 SUTOR CL
18 SADDLERS CL
19 FARRIERS CFT
20 WAGGONERS DR
21 HATTERS CL
22 POTTERS DR
23 WAINERS CL
24 FABER CL
25 CROFT FARM CL
26 GARDENERS CL
27 LORINERS DR
28 FARMERS WY
29 WHEELWRIGHT CL
30 SAWYERS CR
31 THATCHERS CFT
32 HALLCROFT LA

Cemy

EARFIT LA

MOOR LANE

Moor Farm

Copmanthorpe Lodge

STATION

DYKES LA

MAIN ST

BACK LA

PO

Sport Club

Sch

1

HAGG LANE

OLD LA

Copmanthorpe Wood

Copmanthorpe Grange

Greenland Wood

45 Colton Lodge

PH

Lady Flat Farm

PO Colton

54 Lodge Farm

Grange Farm

A 55 B **33** C 56

STREET LANE

COLTON LA

Colton Brock

Brock

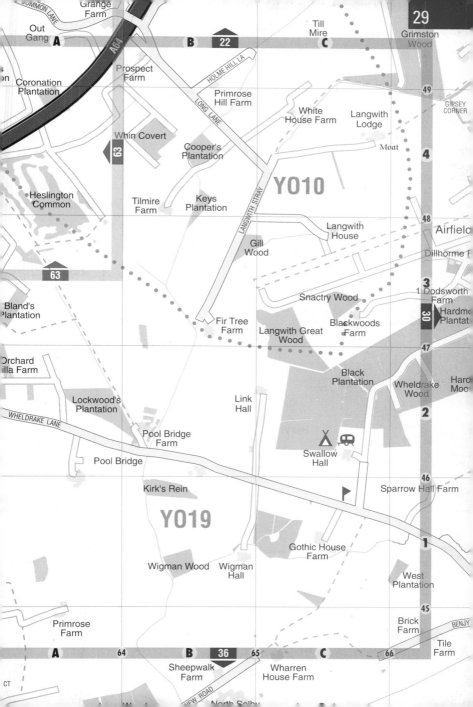

Grange
Farm

COMMON LANE

Out
Gang **A**

Till
Mire

B 22

C

Grimston
Wood

Prospect
Farm

HOLME HILL LA

49

Coronation
Plantation

GIPSEY
CORNER

Primrose
Hill Farm

White
House Farm

Langwith
Lodge

LONG LANE

Whin Covert

4

Moat

63

Cooper's
Plantation

YO10

48

Tilmire
Farm

Keys
Plantation

Heslington
Common

LANGWITH STRAY

Langwith
House

Airfiel

63

Gill
Wood

Dillhorme

Bland's
Plantation

Snactry Wood

3

1 Dodsworth
Farm

Fir Tree
Farm

Langwith Great
Wood

Blackwoods
Farm

30

Hardm
Plantat

Orchard
illa Farm

Langwith Great
Wood

47

Black
Plantation

Wheldrake
Wood

Hard
Moo

Lockwood's
Plantation

Link
Hall

WHELDRAKE LANE

2

Pool Bridge
Farm

Swallow
Hall

Pool Bridge

46

Kirk's Rein

Sparrow Hall Farm

YO19

1

Gothic House
Farm

Wigman Wood

Wigman
Hall

West
Plantation

45

Primrose
Farm

Brick
Farm

BENJY

A 64

B 36 65

C 66

Tile
Farm

Sheepwalk
Farm

Wharren
House Farm

NEW ROAD

CT

North Selby

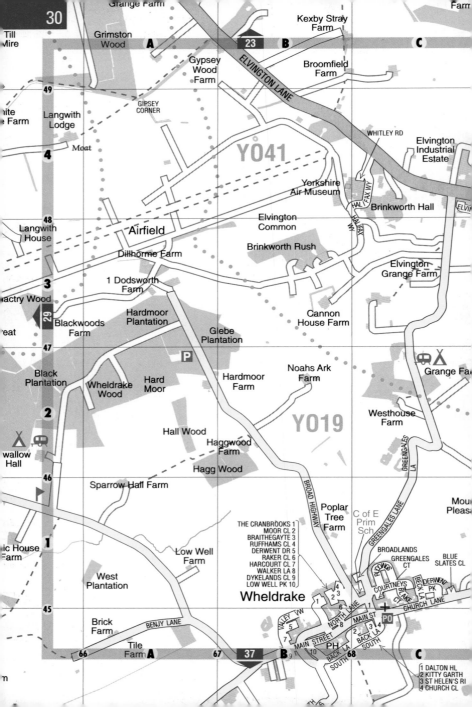

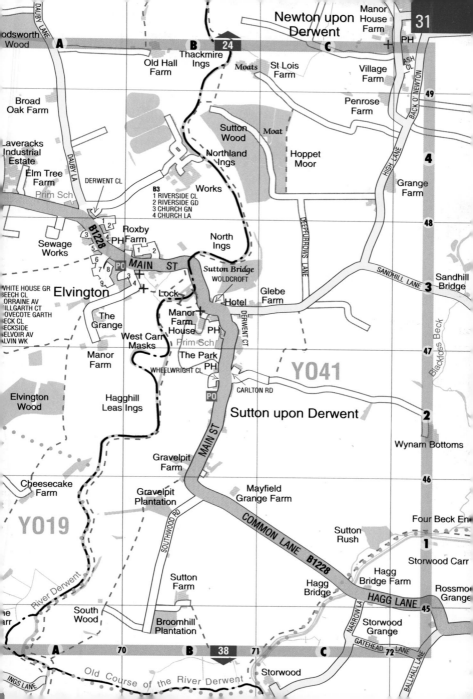

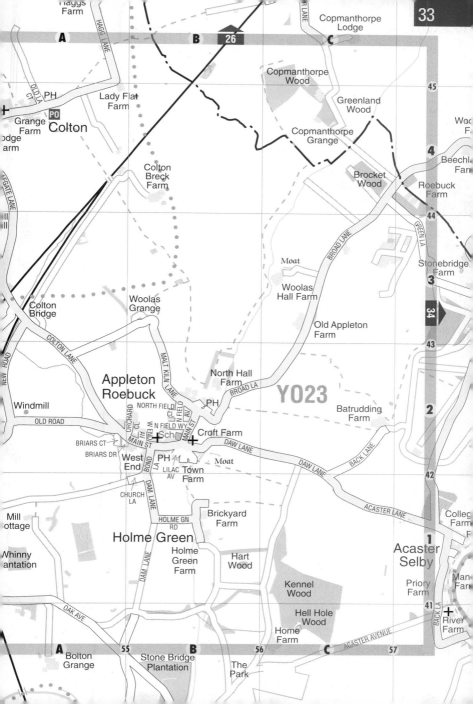

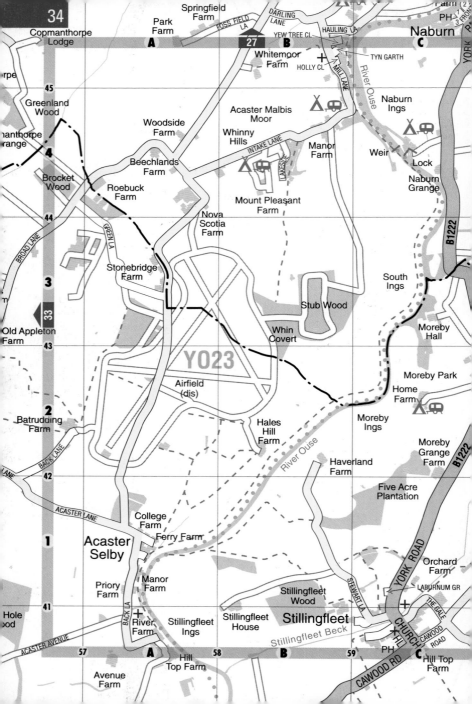

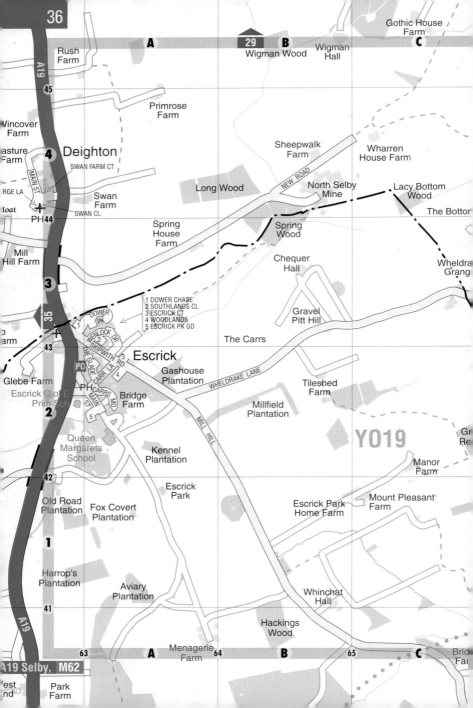

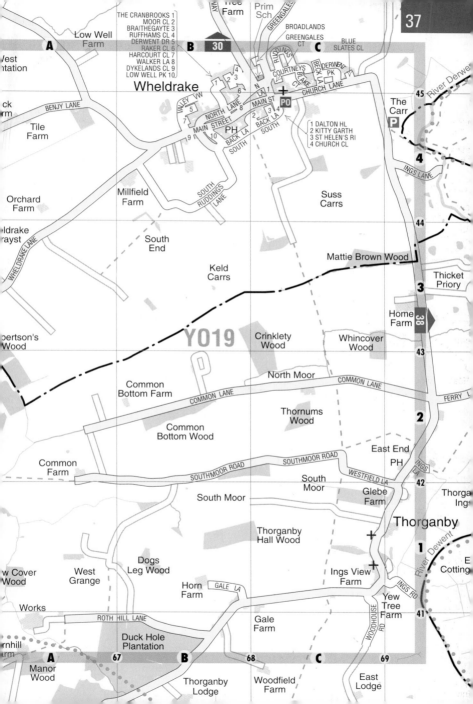

THE CRANBROOKS 1
MOOR CL 2
BRAITHEGAYTE 3
RUFFHAMS CL 4
DERWENT DR 5
HARCOURT CL 7
WALKER LA 8
DYKELANDS CL 9
LOW WELL PK 10

A Low Well Farm

West Plantation

B 30

Prim Sch

BROADLANDS

GREENGALES CT

C BLUE SLATES CL

Wheldrake

BENJY LANE

Tile Farm

VALLEY VW

NORTH LANE

MAIN STREET

PH

BACK LA SOUTH

RUDDINGS

COURTNEYS

BACK LA

DERWENT PK

CHURCH LANE

PO

1 DALTON HL
2 KITTY GARTH
3 ST HELEN'S RI
4 CHURCH CL

The Carr

P

45

River Derwent

Orchard Farm

Millfield Farm

South Ruddings Lane

South End

eldrake rayst

WHELDRAKE LANE

Keld Carrs

Suss Carrs

INGS LANE

44

Mattie Brown Wood

Thicket Priory

3

Home Farm

38

43

robertson's Wood

YO19

Crinkley Wood

Whincover Wood

North Moor

COMMON LANE

FERRY L

Common Bottom Farm

COMMON LANE

Thornums Wood

2

Common Bottom Wood

East End PH

INGS LA

SOUTHMOOR ROAD

Common Farm

SOUTHMOOR ROAD

WESTFIELD LA

42

South Moor

Glebe Farm

South Moor

Thorganby

Thorga Ings

Thorganby Hall Wood

w Cover Wood

West Grange

Dogs Leg Wood

Horn Farm

GALE LA

Ings View Farm

1

River Derwent

E Cotting

Works

ROTH HILL LANE

Gale Farm

Yew Tree Farm

WOODHOUSE RD

INGS RD

41

rnhill arm

A Manor Wood

67

Duck Hole Plantation

B 68

Thorganby Lodge

Woodfield Farm

C 69

East Lodge

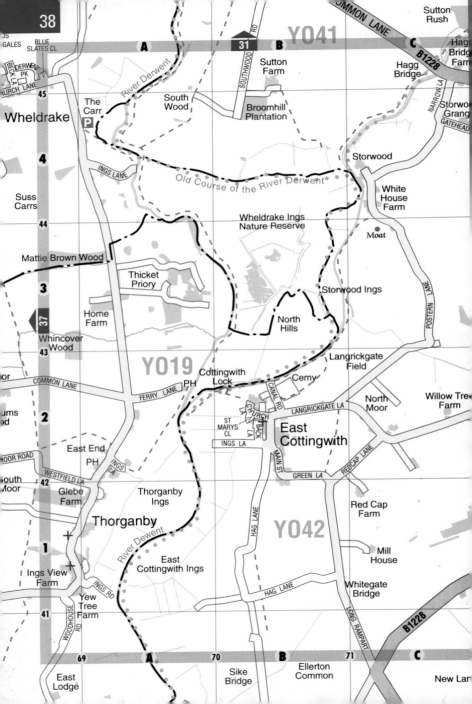

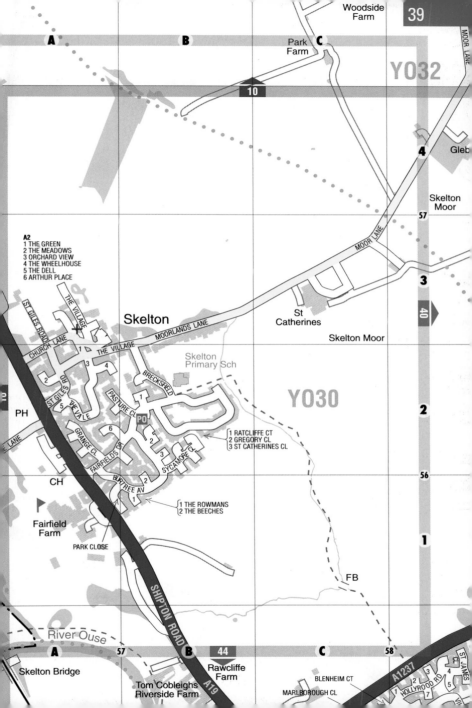

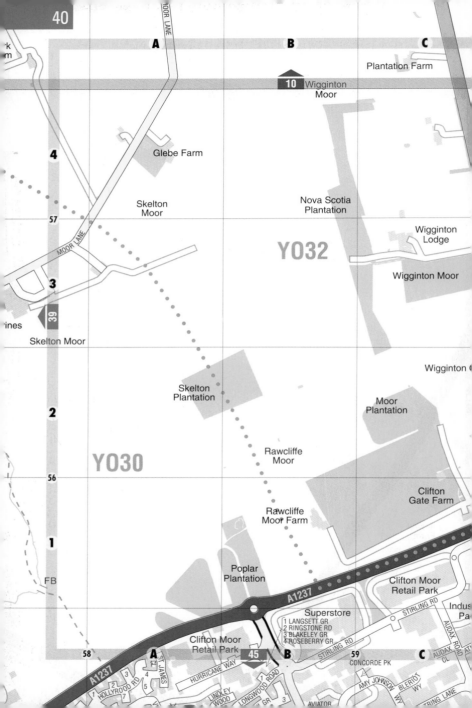

40

A   B   C

Plantation Farm

10 Wigginton Moor

Glebe Farm

4

Skelton Moor

Nova Scotia Plantation

57

Wigginton Lodge

YO32

Moor Lane

Wigginton Moor

3

39

Skelton Moor

ines

Skelton Plantation

Wigginton

Moor Plantation

Rawcliffe Moor

2

YO30

56

Clifton Gate Farm

Rawcliffe Moor Farm

1

FB

Poplar Plantation

Clifton Moor Retail Park

A1237

Superstore
1 LANGSETT GR
2 RINGSTONE RD
3 BLAKELEY GR
4 ROSEBERRY GR

Clifton Moor Retail Park

Industrial Pa

STIRLING RD

58   A   45   B   59   C
Clifton Moor   CONCORDE PK
Retail Park

A1237   ST JAMES

HOLLYROOD RD

HURRICANE WAY

LINDLEY WOOD

LONGWOOD ROAD

AVIATOR

AMY JOHNSON WY

BLERIOT WY

STRING LANE

AUDAX ROAD

AUDAX CL

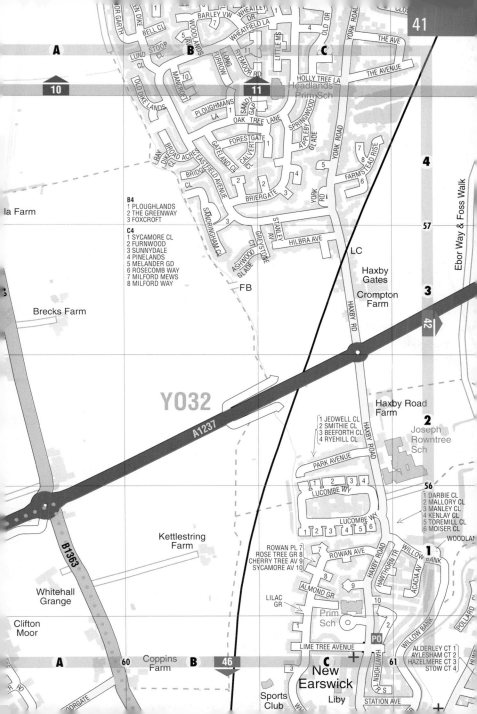

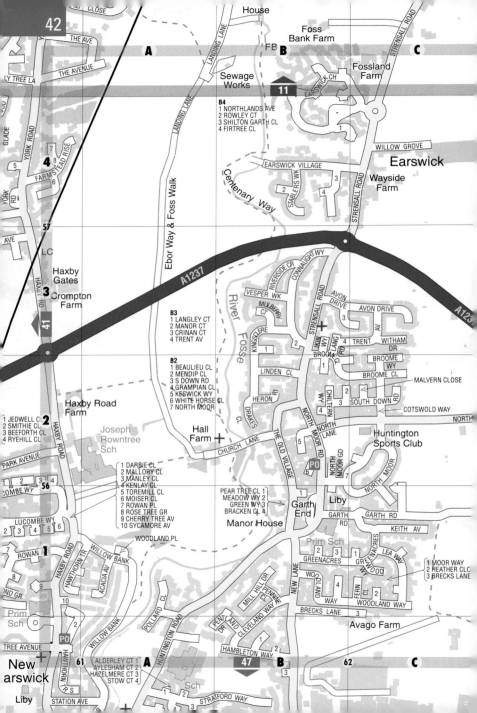

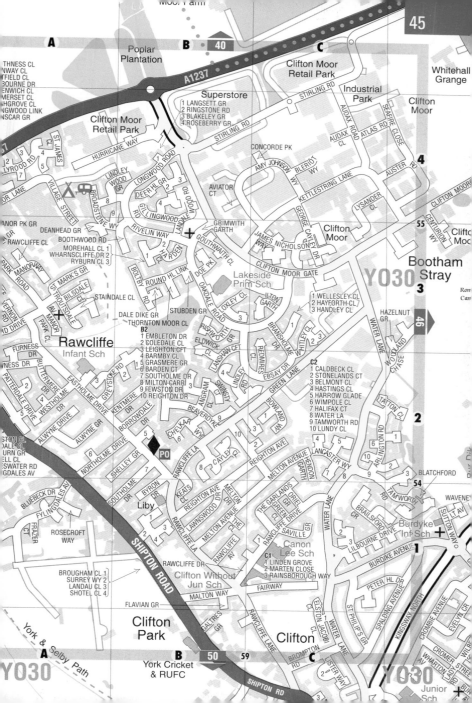

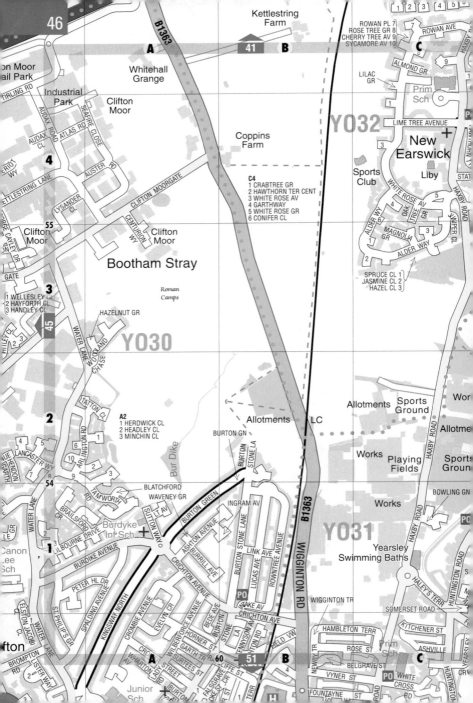

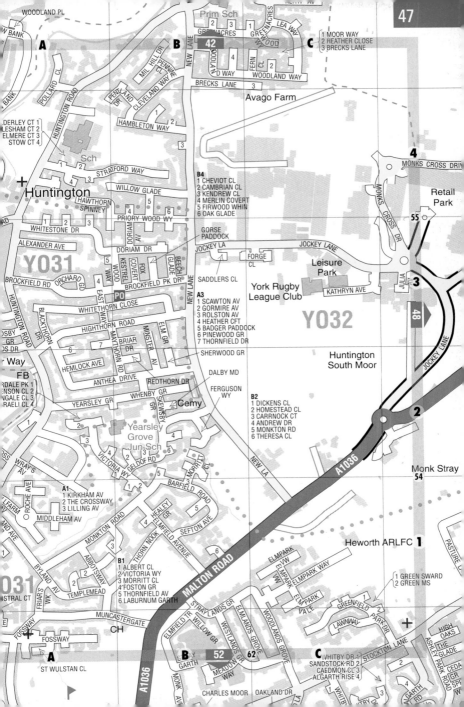

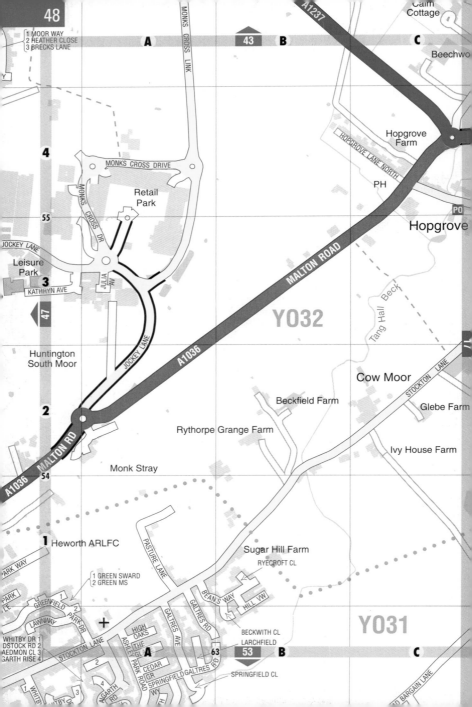

1 MOOR WAY
2 HEATHER CLOSE
3 BRECKS LANE

A

43

B

C

Cairn Cottage

Beechwo

4

MONKS CROSS DRIVE

Retail Park

MONKS CROSS DR

55

JOCKEY LANE

Leisure Park

3

KATHRYN AVE

JULIA AV

47

Huntington South Moor

MONKS CROSS LINK

A1237

Hopgrove Farm

HOPGROVE LANE NORTH

PH

PO

Hopgrove

MALTON ROAD

YO32

Tang Hall Beck

JOCKEY LANE

A1036

Cow Moor

STOCKTON LANE

Glebe Farm

2

MALTON RD

Beckfield Farm

Rythorpe Grange Farm

Ivy House Farm

A1036

54

Monk Stray

1 Heworth ARLFC

PASTURE LANE

Sugar Hill Farm

RYECROFT CL

ARK WAY

1 GREEN SWARD
2 GREEN MS

1

GREENFIELD

PARK DR

BEAN'S WAY

HILL VW

PARK

LAWNWAY

STOCKTON LANE

HIGH OAKS

GALTRES AVE

GALTRES RD

YO31

WHITBY DR 1
DSTOCK RD 2
AEDMON CL 3
GARTH RISE 4

ASHLEY PARK ROAD

THE GL

CEDAR GR

A

63

53

B

C

BECKWITH CL
LARCHFIELD

ALGARTH RD

SPRINGFIELD GALTRES RD

SPRINGFIELD CL

WY

WHITB

D BARGAIN LANE

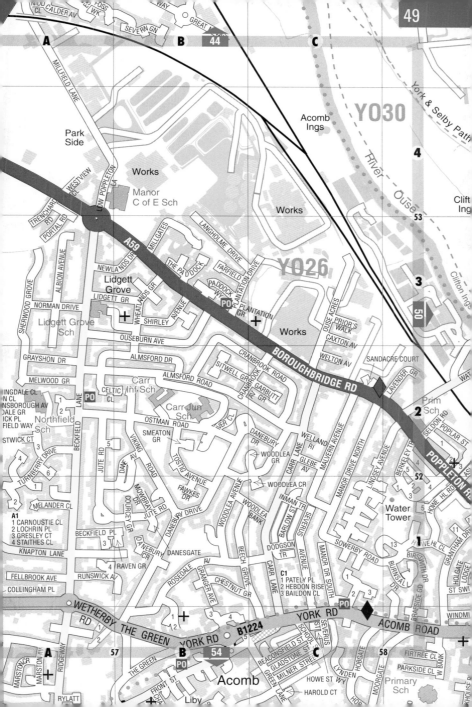

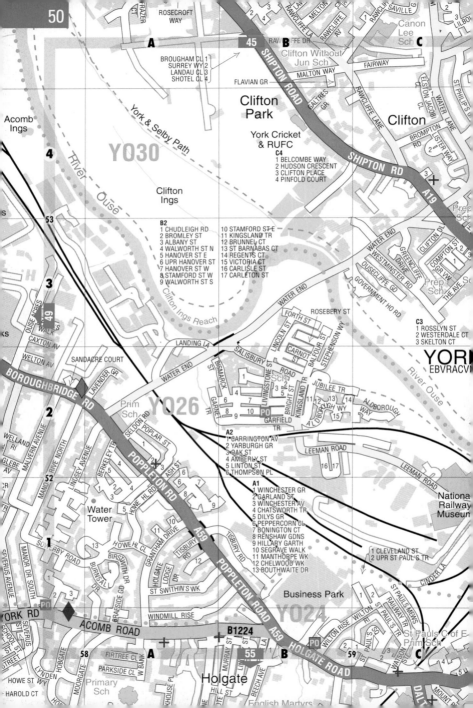

ROSECROFT WAY
FRAZER CT

45 Rawcliffe Dr
W
C
Canon
Lee
Sch

BROUGHAM CL 1
SURREY WY 2
LANDAU CL 3
SHOTEL CL 4

Clifton Without
Jun Sch
FAIRWAY

FLAVIAN GR
MALTON WAY

SHIPTON ROAD
GALTRES GR

RAWCLIFFE LANE

Clifton

Clifton Park

WATER END

York Cricket
& RUFC

SHIPTON RD

BROMPTON RD

Acomb
Ings

YO30

C4
1 BELCOMBE WAY
2 HUDSON CRESCENT
3 CLIFTON PLACE
4 PINFOLD COURT

A19

Prep
Sch

4

River Ouse

York & Selby Path

Clifton
Ings

WATER END

WESTMINSTER
DRIVE

CLIFTON DV

GREENCLIFFE
DRIVE

OUSECLIFFE GD

GOVERNMENT HO RD

Prep
Sch

THE AVE

COMPTON ST

GR VW

53

B2
1 CHUDLEIGH RD
2 BROMLEY ST
3 ALBANY ST
4 WALWORTH ST N
5 HANOVER ST E
6 UPR HANOVER ST
7 HANOVER ST W
8 STAMFORD ST W
9 WALWORTH ST S

10 STAMFORD ST E
11 KINGSLAND TR
12 BRUNNEL CT
13 ST BARNABAS CT
14 REGENTS CT
15 VICTORIA CT
16 CARLISLE ST
17 CARLETON ST

3

Ouse Acres
WALK

49

Clifton Ings Reach

CAXTON AV

WELTON AV

LANDING LA

WATER END

ROSEBERY ST

FORTH ST

C3
1 ROSSLYN ST
2 WESTERDALE CT
3 SKELTON CT

YOR
EBVRACV

River Ouse

SANDACRE COURT

LAVENDER GR

BOROUGHBRIDGE RD

YO26

Prim
Sch

SALISBURY

BISMARCK ST

GARNET

ROAD

LINCOLN ST

CARNOT
ST

BALFOUR ST

STEPHENSON WY

JUBILEE TR

ALDBOROUGH
WAY

2

WELLAND
RI

GLEBE
AV

MALVERN AVENUE

BERKELEY TR

SELDON RD

POPLAR ST

POPPLETON RD

ASH ST

LIVINGSTONE ST

BRIGHT ST

KINGSLAND TER

SchT

OLDBOROUGH WY

ALDBOROUGH WY

GARFIELD
TR

A2
1 CARRINGTON AV
2 YARBURGH GR
3 OAK ST
4 AMBERLY ST
5 LINTON ST
6 THOMPSON PL

LEEMAN ROAD

LEEMAN ROAD

52

LINDSEY AVENUE

MANOR DRIVE NORTH

HOME HL RD

GRANTHAM DRIVE

A59

A1
1 WINCHESTER GR
2 GARLAND ST
3 WINCHESTER AV
4 CHATSWORTH TR
5 DILYS GR
6 PEPPERCORN GL
7 BONINGTON CT
8 RENSHAW GDNS
9 HILLARY GARTH
10 SEGRAVE WALK
11 MANTHORPE WK
12 CHELWOOD WK
13 BOUTHWAITE DR

Nationa
Railway
Museum

**Water
Tower**

HOWE HL CL

BIRSWITH DR

BURNSALL DR

HOLGATE
LODGE

TISBURY
RD

1 CLEVELAND ST
2 UPR ST PAUL'S TR

ST PAUL'S MEWS

CINDER LA

1

SOWERBY ROAD

MANOR DR SOUTH

SEVERUS AVENUE

BRACKSIDE GD

ST SWITHIN'S WK

WINDMILL RISE

Business Park

WILTON RISE

RAILWAY TR

ST PAUL'S TR

HOLGATE

PO

YO24

St Pauls C of E
Prim Sch

YORK RD

PO

ACOMB ROAD

B1224

55
B

HOLGATE ROAD

POPPLETON ROAD

A59

PO

59
C

SEVERUS

SCHOOL ST

STREET

HOBGATE

MOORGATE

FIRTREE CL

PARKSIDE CL

HOUSE PL

HILL ST

BEECH AV

WILTON RISE

ST PAUL'S SQ

DALT

MOUNT

58
A

Holgate

LYNDEN

HOWE ST WY

HAROLD CT

Primary
Sch

English Martyrs

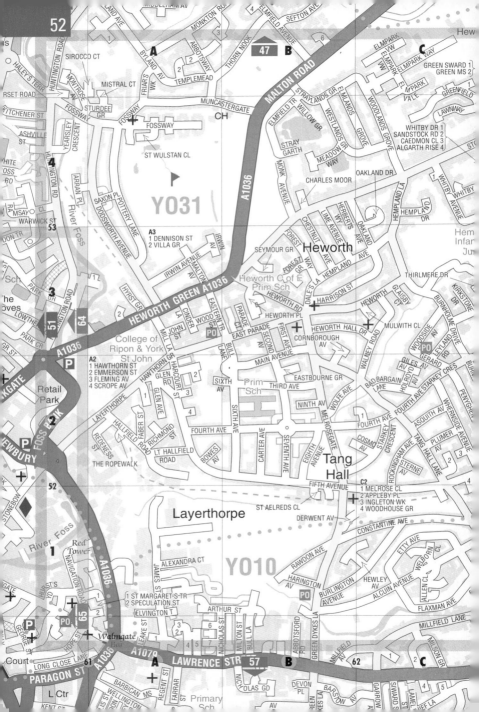

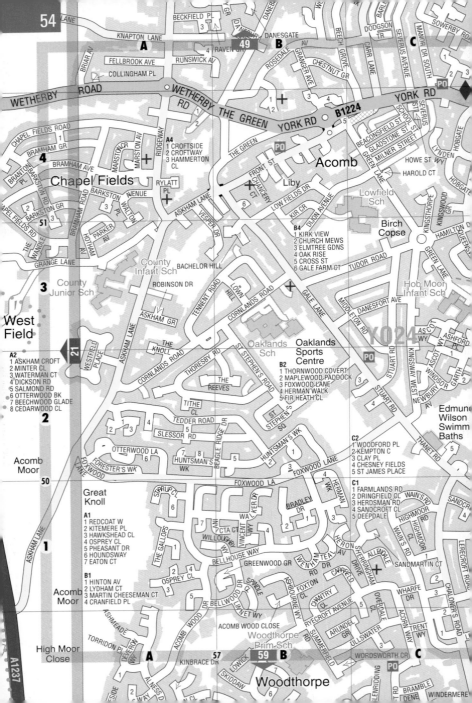

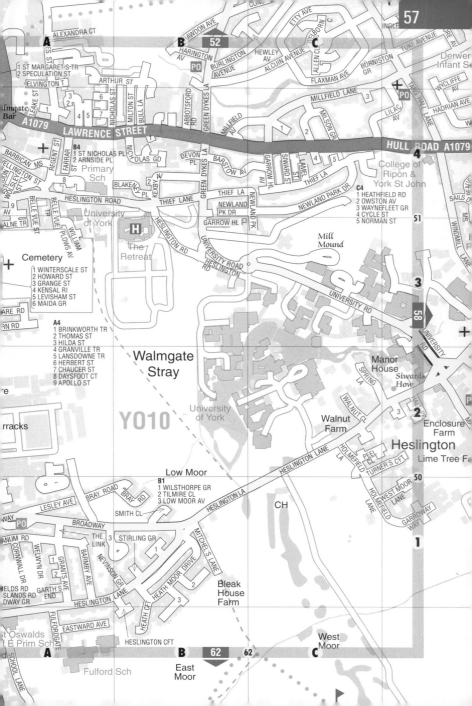

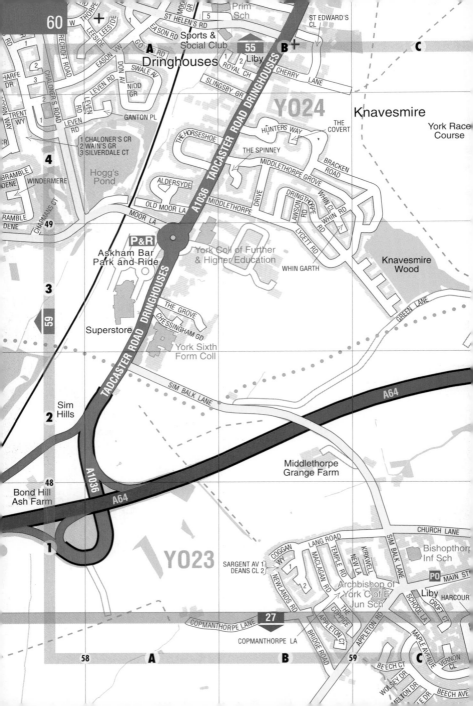

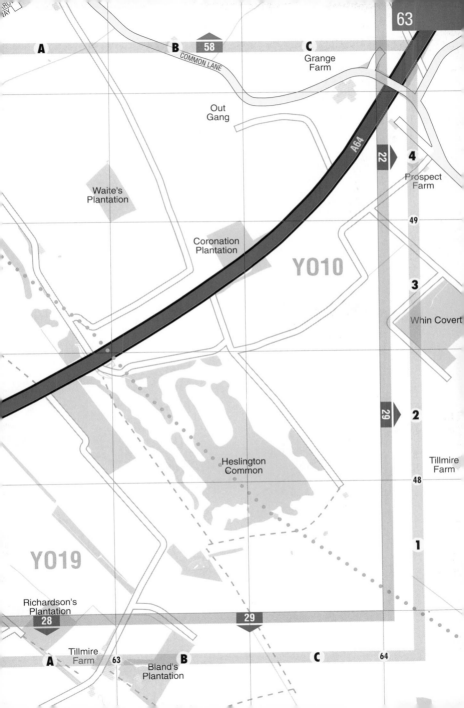

Scale: 7 inches to 1 mile
0 — 110 yards — 220 yards
0 — 125 m — 250 m

52
525
51
50
525

River Foss
HUNTINGTON ROAD
DENNISON STREET
DALGUISE GROVE
MONKBRIDGE COURT
NEWORTH GN
GLADSTONE STREET
GROVE LANE
PARK GROVE
LOWTHER COURT
FOSS BANK
A1036
FOSS ISL
Retail Park
Industrial Estate
Ind Est
GRAY'S CV
ELDON TR
STANLEY STREET
NELSON
NEVILLE TERR
AMBER ST
DUDLEY ST
PARK CRES
GROVES LANE
GEORGE CT
AGAR ST
MONKGATE
THE CLOISTERS
City Wall
JEWBURY
A1036
MARKHAM STREET
MARKHAM CRESCENT
NEVILLE STREET
ELDON STREET
JACKSON ST
BROWNLOW ST
Pk Grove Sch
PENLEY'S GROVE STREET
GARDEN STREET
KINGS SQUARE
OAKWOOD
WAVERLEY
ST JOHN STREET
MONKGATE CLOISTERS
Monk Bar
St Maurice's Rd
Merchant Taylors Hall
HAXBY ROAD
ST THOMAS'S PLACE
TOWNEND STREET
GARDEN PLACE
DE GREY STREET
St Wilfrids RC Prim Sch
Richard III Mus
St William's College
York Minster
Minster Library
Treasurer's House
WIGGINTON ROAD
B1363
CLARENCE STREET
BROOK STREET
LORD MAYOR'S WALK
A1036
YORK
YO31
College of Ripon & York St John
UNION TERRACE
CLAREMONT TERR
GILLYGATE
DE GREY TERRACE
CITY WALL
A1036
Bootham Bar
The Purey Cust Nuffield
Minster Yard
Gatehouse
Dean's Park
York District
Bootham Park
Gate
PORTLAND STREET
BOOTHAM ROW
Theatre Royal
ST LEONARD'S PL
Assembly Rooms
SCARBOROUGH TR
BRIDGE LANE
Bootham Sch
PERCY ST
York City Art Gallery
Exhibition Square
Central Library
GILLYGATE
NEWBOROUGH ST
YORK CITY FOOTBALL CLUB
GROSVENOR ROAD
GROSVENOR TERRACE
ST OLAVE'S ROAD
BOOTHAM CRESCENT
BOOTHAM
A19
Abbey
University of York
Yorkshire Museum
Museum Gardens
The Hospitium
Observatory
Tower
AVENUE RD
AVENUE TERRACE
PETERSWAY
BURTON STONE LANE
ST PETER'S GROVE
QUEEN ANNE ROAD
NORTH PARADE
CLIFTON ROAD
A19
YO30
St Peters Sch
St Olave's Sch
Clifton Prep Sch
MARYGATE
ST MARY'S
MARYGATE LANE
FREDERIC STREET
SYCAMORE PL
SYCAMORE TERRACE
LONGFIELD TERRACE
BOOTHAM TERRACE
ALMERY TR
ST MARY'S TERR
Tower

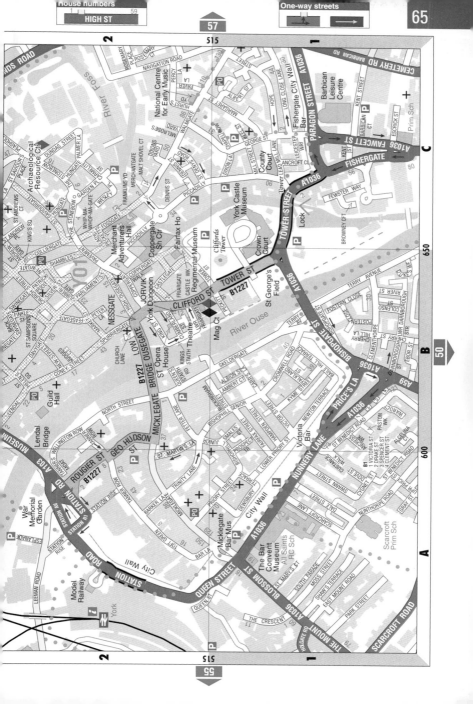

Index

Street names are listed alphabetically and show the locality, the Postcode District, the page number and a reference to the square in which the name falls on the map page

Church La **4** Elvington YO41...............**31** B3

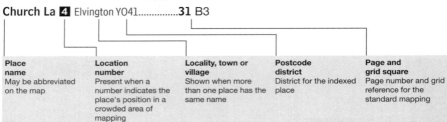

Place name	Location number	Locality, town or village	Postcode district	Page and grid square
May be abbreviated on the map	Present when a number indicates the place's position in a crowded area of mapping	Shown when more than one place has the same name	District for the indexed place	Page number and grid reference for the standard mapping

Public and commercial buildings are highlighted in magenta. **Places of interest** are highlighted in blue with a star*

Abbreviations used in the index

Acad	**Academy**	Comm	**Common**	Gd	**Ground**	L	**Leisure**	Prom	**Prom**
App	**Approach**	Cott	**Cottage**	Gdn	**Garden**	La	**Lane**	Rd	**Road**
Arc	**Arcade**	Cres	**Crescent**	Gn	**Green**	Liby	**Library**	Recn	**Recreation**
Ave	**Avenue**	Cswy	**Causeway**	Gr	**Grove**	Mdw	**Meadow**	Ret	**Retail**
Bglw	**Bungalow**	Ct	**Court**	H	**Hall**	Meml	**Memorial**	Sh	**Shopping**
Bldg	**Building**	Ctr	**Centre**	Ho	**House**	Mkt	**Market**	Sq	**Square**
Bsns, Bus	**Business**	Ctry	**Country**	Hospl	**Hospital**	Mus	**Museum**	St	**Street**
Bvd	**Boulevard**	Cty	**County**	HQ	**Headquarters**	Orch	**Orchard**	Sta	**Station**
Cath	**Cathedral**	Dr	**Drive**	Hts	**Heights**	Pal	**Palace**	Terr	**Terrace**
Cir	**Circus**	Dro	**Drove**	Ind	**Industrial**	Par	**Parade**	TH	**Town Hall**
Cl	**Close**	Ed	**Education**	Inst	**Institute**	Pas	**Passage**	Univ	**University**
Cnr	**Corner**	Emb	**Embankment**	Int	**International**	Pk	**Park**	Wk, Wlk	**Walk**
Coll	**College**	Est	**Estate**	Intc	**Interchange**	Pl	**Place**	Wr	**Water**
Com	**Community**	Ex	**Exhibition**	Junc	**Junction**	Prec	**Precinct**	Yd	**Yard**

Index of localities, towns and villages

Acaster Malbis 27 C1
Acaster Selby 34 A1
Acomb 54 B4
Angram 25 B4
Appleton Roebuck ...33 B2
Askham Bryan 26 B4
Askham Richard 25 C4

Beningbrough 8 C1
Bilbrough 25 C2
Bishopthorpe 27 C3
Bolton Percy 32 C1
Bootham Stray 46 A3
Bossall 14 C4
Brockfield 18 A3

Catterton 25 A1
Chapel Fields 54 A4
Claxton 14 A4

Clifton 50 C4
Clifton Park 50 B4
Cock Hill 15 A3
Colton 33 A4
Copmanthorpe 26 B2
Crockey Hill 28 C2
Cross Lanes 2 C4

Deighton 35 C4
Dringhouses 55 A1
Dunnington 23 B4

Earswick 42 C4
East Cottingwith ..38 B2
Elvington 31 A3
Escrick 36 A2

Flaxton 7 B2
Fulford 62 A4

Gate Helmsley 19 A3
Grimston 22 B3
Hall Garth 23 B3
Haxby 11 A1
Heslington 58 A2
Hessay 15 B1
Heworth 52 B3
High Catton 19 C1
Holgate 55 B4
Holme Green 33 B1
Holtby 18 B2
Hopgrove 48 C3
Huby 3 C4
Huntington 47 A4
Hutton Wandesley ..20 A2

Kexby 24 B3
Knapton 21 C4
Knavesmire 60 C4

Layerthorpe 52 A1
Long Marston 20 A3
Low Catton 19 B1

Middlethorpe 61 A3
Murton 22 C4

Naburn 27 C1
Nether
  Poppleton 16 C2
New Earswick 46 C4
Newton-on-Ouse ...8 A3
Nunthorpe 56 B1

Osbaldwick 53 B1
Overton 16 B3

Rawcliffe 45 A3
Rufforth 20 B3

Sand Hutton 14 A2
Shipton 9 B2
Skelton 39 B3
South Bank 56 A2
Stamford Bridge ..19 C3
Stillingfleet 34 B1
Stockton on the
  Forest 17 C4
Street Houses 25 B1
Strensall 11 C4
Strensall Camp ...12 A3
Sutton upon Derwent .31 B2
Sutton-on-the-
  Forest 4 B4

Tang Hall 52 B2
Thorganby 38 A1
Thornton-le-Clay ..7 C4
Tollerton 2 A4

Towthorpe 12 C4

Upper Helmsley ...19 A4
Upper Poppleton ..16 B2

Walmgate Stray ...57 B2
Warthill 18 B3
West Field 21 C2
West Lilling 6 B4
Wheldrake 30 B1
Wigginton 10 C2
Woodthorpe 59 B4

York 64 B3

A

Abbey St YO30 ....50 C4
Abbotsford Rd YO10 ...57 B4
Abbot St YO11 ....64 C4
Abbotsway YO31 ....47 A1
Abelton Gr 32 YO32 ...11 A2
Acacia Ave YO31 ....42 A1
Acaster La
Acaster Malbis YO23 ...27 C2
Acaster Selby YO23 ...33 C1
Acomb Prim Sch YO24 54 A4
Acomb Rd YO24 ....54 C4
Acomb Wood Cl YO24 ...59 A4
Acomb Wood Dr YO24 59 A4
Acorn Way YO24 ....59 C4
Adelaide St 3 YO23 ...56 A3
Adlington Cl 8 YO32 ..11 C4
Agar St YO31 ....64 C3
Ainsty Ave YO26 ...55 B1
Ainsty Gr YO24 ....55 B1
Aintree Ct YO24 ....55 B1
Albany St 3 YO26 ....50 B2
Albemarle Rd YO23 ...56 A3
Albert Cl 1 YO32 ...47 B1
Albert St YO10 ....65 A1
Albion Ave YO26 ...49 A3
Albion St YO1 ....65 B1
Alcelina Ct YO23 ....65 B1
Alcuin Ave YO10 ...52 C1
Aldborough Way YO26 50 B2
Alderley Ct YO24 ....47 A4
Aldersyde YO24 ....60 A4
Alder Way YO32 ....46 C3
Aldreth Gr YO23 ....56 B3
Aldwark YO1 ....64 C3
Alexander Ave YO31 ...47 A3
Alexandra Ct YO10 ...52 A1
Alexandra Rd YO32 ...11 C3
Algarth Rd YO31 ....53 A4
Algarth Rise YO31 ...53 A4
Allan St 1 YO30 ...51 B4
Allen Cl YO10 ....52 C1
Allendale YO24 ....54 C1
Allerton Dr
22 Poppleton YO26 ...16 B2
Poppleton YO26 ....16 C2
Allington Dr YO31 ...53 A3
Allotments La YO61 ...3 B4
All Saints RC Comp Sch
YO24 ....65 A1
Alma Terr YO10 ....56 C3
Almery Terr YO30 ...64 A3
Almond Gr YO32 ....41 C1
Almsford Dr YO26 ...49 B2
Almsford Rd YO26 ...49 B2
Alness Dr YO24 ....59 A4
Alne Terr YO10 ....57 A2
Alvin Wlk 3 YO41 ...31 A3
Alvis Gr YO31 ....53 C1
Alwyne Dr YO30 ....45 A2
Alwyne Gr YO30 ....45 A2
Amberly St 4 YO26 ...50 A2
Amber St YO31 ....64 C4
Ambler's La YO30 ...9 B4
Ambleside Ave YO10 ...53 A1
Ambrose St YO10 ....56 C2
Ancholme Way
YO30 ....45 C4
Ancress Wlk YO10 ...65 B1
Ancroft Cl YO31 ....65 C1
Anderson Gr 6 YO25 55 B3
Andrew Dr 4 YO32 ...47 B2
Angram Cl YO30 ....45 B2
Angram La YO61 ....2 A4
Annan Cl YO10 ....45 C4
Anne St YO23 ....56 B3
Anson Dr YO10 ....56 C1
Anthea Dr YO31 ....47 A2
Apollo St 3 YO10 ...57 A4
Appleby Glade YO32 ...41 C4
Appleby Pl 2 YO31 ...52 C2
Applecroft Rd YO31 ...53 A4
Appleby Garth 3 YO30 16 B2
Appleton Ct YO23 ....27 B3
Appleton Rd YO23 ...27 C3
Appleton Roebuck CP Sch
YO23 ....33 C1
Archaeological
Centre* YO1 ....65 C2
Archbishop Holgates Sch
YO10 ....58 A4
Archbishop of York C of E
Jun Sch YO23 ....60 C1
Arenhall Cl 10 YO32 ...11 A1
Argyle St YO23 ....56 A2
Arlington Rd YO30 ...45 C2
Arnside Pl 2 YO10 ...57 B4
Arran Pl YO31 ....51 C4
Arran Pl 17 YO30 ....39 A2
Arthur St YO10 ....52 A1
Arundel Gr YO24 ....59 B4
Ascot Way YO24 ....54 B1
Ashbourne Way YO24 54 B1
Ash Cl YO31 ....53 A4
Ashdale Rd 16 YO32 23 B4
Ashford Pl YO24 ....59 A4
Ash La 8 YO32 ....11 A2

Ashley Park Cres YO31 53 A3
Ashley Park Rd YO31 ...53 A3
Ashmeade Cl YO24 ...54 A1
Ash St YO26 ....50 A1
Ashton Ave YO30 ....46 A1
Ashville St YO31 ....51 C4
Ashwood Glade YO32 41 B3
Askham Bryan Coll
YO23 ....26 B3
Askham Croft YO24 54 A2
Askham Fields La
YO23 ....55 B4
Askham Gr YO24 ....54 A3
Askham La YO24 ....54 A3
Aspen Cl 3 YO19 ...23 B4
Asquith Ave YO31 ....51 B2
Atcherley Cl YO10 ...56 C1
Atlas Rd YO30 ....45 C4
Audax Cl YO30 ....45 C4
Audax Cl YO30 ....45 C4
Auster Rd YO30 ....46 A4
Avenue Rd YO30 ....46 A4
Avenue Terr YO30 ....64 A4
Avenue The
32 Haxby YO32 ....11 A1
1 Haxby YO32 ....11 A2
Rufforth YO23 ....20 B3
York YO30 ....50 C3
Aviator Ct YO30 ....45 B4
Avon Dr YO32 ....41 A3
Aylesham Ct YO32 ...47 A4

B

Bachelor Hill YO24 ...54 B3
Backhouse St YO31 ...64 B4
Back La
Appleton Roebuck YO23 33 C2
Bilbrough YO23 ....25 C2
Copmanthorpe YO23 ...26 C2
Cottingwith YO42 ....38 B2
Flaxton YO60 ....7 C2
1 Haxby YO32 ....11 A1
Holtby YO19 ....18 A1
Newton-on-Ouse YO30 12 A4
Back La S YO23 ....37 B4
Back YO26 ....21 C4
Back Swinegate YO1 ...65 B1
Bad Bargain La YO31 ...52 C2
Badger Hill Prim Sch
YO10 ....58 A3
Badger Paddock 5
YO31 ....47 A3
Badger Wood Wlk YO10
....58 C4
Baildon Cl 3 YO26 ...49 C1
Bale Hill Terr YO1 ....65 B1
Baker St YO31 ....64 C4
Balfour St YO26 ....50 B2
Balfour Way YO32 ....41 C3
Balmoral Terr 5 YO23 56 A2
Bankside Cl 3 YO26 ...16 B2
Bannisdale 4 YO24 ...59 B4
Barbara Gr 4 YO26 ...55 B2
Barbers Dr
1 Copmanthorpe YO23 26 C3
Copmanthorpe YO23 ...59 A1
Barbican Ct YO10 ....65 C1
Barbican Leisure Ctr
YO10 ....65 C1
Barbican Mews YO10 ...57 A4
Barbican Rd YO10 ....65 C1
Barden Ct YO31 ....46 B3
Barfield Rd YO31 ....47 B1
Barker La YO1 ....65 A1
Barkston Ave YO26 ...54 A4
Barkston Cl 3 YO26 ...21 C3
Barkston Gr 3 YO26 ...21 C3
Barkston Rd YO26 ...21 C3
Bar La YO1 ....65 A2
Barley Rise YO32 ....11 C3
Barley View 18 YO32 ...11 C3
Barlow St YO26 ....49 C1
Barmby Ave YO10 ....57 C1
Barmby Cl 4 YO30 ...45 B2
Barney La YO60 ....7 C2
Barnfield Way 14 YO23 56 B3
Barons Cres YO23 ....26 C2
Barrett Ave 3 YO26 ...55 B4
Barstow Ave YO10 ....57 B4
Bartle Garth YO1 ....64 C3
Bateson Cl YO30 ....58 B2
Battleflats Way YO41 ...19 C3
Baysdale Ave YO10 ...58 C4
Beadle Garth YO24 ...54 C4
Beagle Croft YO41 ....19 B2
Beagle Ridge Dr YO24 ...54 B2
Beagle Spinney YO41 ...19 B2
Beanland La YO32 ....17 C3
Bean's Way YO31 ....48 A1
Beaufort Cl 3 YO24 ...59 B4
Beaulieu Cl 1 YO32 ...42 B2
Beaverdyke YO30 ....45 A1
Beck Cl 6 YO32 ....31 A3

Beckfield La YO26 ....49 A2
Beckfield Pl YO26 ....49 A1
Beck La YO19 ....30 C1
Becks Cl 8 YO32 ....11 A1
Beckside 4 YO41 ....31 A3
Beckwith Cl YO31 ....53 B4
Bedale Ave YO31 ....53 C1
Bede Ave YO30 ....51 A4
Bedern YO1 ....64 C3
Beech Ave
Bishopthorpe YO23 ...27 C3
York YO31 ....55 B4
Beech Cl 3 YO41 ....31 A3
Beech Cl 4 YO23 ....27 C3
Beeches The YO30 ...39 B1
Beechfield YO10 ....8 A3
Beech Glade YO31 ...47 B3
Beech Gr YO26 ....49 B1
Beech Pl 8 YO31 ....11 C1
Beechwood Glade 7
YO24 ....54 A2
Beeforth Cl YO32 ....42 A2
Belcombe Way 1
YO30 ....50 C4
Belgrave St YO31 ....51 B4
Bell Cl 7 YO32 ....42 A2
Belle Vue St YO10 ....57 A4
Belle Vue Terr YO10 ...57 A4
Belfarm Ave YO31 ....47 A1
Bellground La YO30 ...8 C1
Bellhouse Way YO24 ...54 A1
Bellmans Croft 7
YO23 ....26 C2
Bellwood Dr YO24 ...54 A1
Belmont Cl 3 YO30 ...45 C2
Belvoir Ave YO41 ....31 A3
Benningbrough La YO30 8 C2
Benjy La YO19 ....37 A4
Beresford Terr YO23 ...56 B2
Berkeley Terr YO26 ...50 B2
Beverley Balk YO41 ...19 A3
Bewlay St YO23 ....56 B3
Bilsdale Cl YO10 ....45 A3
Birch La 8 YO32 ....11 A2
Birkdale Gr YO26 ....49 A2
Birker La YO19 ....24 C1
Birstwith Dr YO26 ...50 A1
Bishopgate St YO23 ...65 B1
Bishophill Jun YO1 ...65 A1
Bishophill Senior YO1 ...65 A1
Bishopsway YO10 ....58 B4
Bishopthorpe Inf Sch
YO23 ....60 C1
Bishopthorpe Pal*
YO23 ....61 A1
Bishopthorpe Rd YO23 61 A2
Bismarck St YO26 ....50 A2
Black Dike La YO26 ...16 B1
Blackless Cl 3 YO42 ...6 A1
Blackthorn Dr YO31 ...53 A4
Blake Ct YO19 ....30 C1
Blakeley Gr YO30 ....45 B4
Blakeney Pl YO31 ....51 C4
Blake St YO1 ....65 B2
Bland La YO26 ....21 C3
Blatchford YO24 ....46 A1
Blenheim St YO31 ....64 B4
Bleriot Way YO30 ....45 C4
Blossom St YO24 ....65 A1
Blue Bridge La YO10 ...56 C3
Blue Slates Cl YO19 ...24 C1
Bog La YO10 ....58 B4
Bollans Ct YO1 ....64 C3
Boltby Rd YO30 ....45 B3
Bond La YO23 ....21 C3
Bonington Ct 7 YO26 50 A1
Bootham Bar* YO31 ...64 B3
Bootham Cres YO30 ...64 A4
Bootham Park Hospl
YO30 ....64 B4
Bootham Row YO31 ...64 B3
Bootham Sq YO31 ....64 B3
Bootham Terr YO30 ...64 A3
Bootham YO30 ....64 A3
Boothwood Rd YO30 ...45 A3
Bore Tree Baulk YO32 ...6 A4
Boroughbridge Rd
YO26 ....49 C2
Borrowdale Dr YO10 ...58 C4
Bouthwaite Dr 12
YO26 ....50 A1
Bowes Ave YO31 ....53 A4
Bowland Way YO30 ...45 C4
Bowling Green Ct
YO10 ....46 C1
Bowling Green La
YO23 ....64 C1
Bowness Dr YO31 ....53 A4
Bowyers Cl YO23 ....59 B1
Bracken Cl YO32 ....42 B1
Brackenhills YO26 ....16 B2
Bracken Hill 2 YO10 ...58 B4
Bracken Rd YO24 ....60 B4
Bradley Cres YO23 ....26 C2
Bradley Dr YO24 ....59 B4
Bradley La YO23 ....20 B2
Beck YO24 ....52 C4

Braegate La LS24 ....33 A4
Braeside Gdns YO10 ...58 B3
Brailsford Cres YO30 ...45 C1
Braithegayte YO19 ....30 B1
Bramble Dene YO24 ...59 C4
Bramham Ave YO26 ...21 C3
Bramham Gr YO26 ...21 C3
Bramham Rd YO26 ...21 C2
Bramley Garth YO31 ...53 A3
Brandon Gr YO32 ....17 B3
Brandsby Gr YO31 ....52 A3
Bransdale Cres YO10 ...58 C4
Bransholme Dr YO30 ...45 C2
Branton Pl 3 YO26 ...21 C3
Breary Cl YO30 ....39 B1
Bray Rd YO10 ....57 B1
Breary La YO23 ....26 C2
Brecksfield YO30 ....39 B2
Brecks La
Strensall YO32 ....12 A4
York YO32 ....42 B1
Brentwood Cres YO10 58 B3
Briar Ave YO26 ....55 A4
Briar Dr YO31 ....47 B3
Briars Cl YO23 ....33 A2
Briars Dr YO23 ....33 A2
Bridge Cl YO24 ....41 B4
Bridge La YO30 ....64 B4
Bridge La YO19 ....23 B4
Bridge Rd YO23 ....27 B3
Bridle Way 1 YO26 ...54 B1
Bridlington Rd 1
YO13 ....19 C3
Briergate YO32 ....41 B4
Briggs St YO31 ....51 B4
Bright St YO26 ....50 A2
Brinkworth Terr 1
YO10 ....57 A4
Broad Acres YO32 ....41 B4
Broad Highway YO19 ...30 B1
Broad La
Appleton Roebuck YO23 33 C3
Catton YO41 ....24 B4
Broadlands YO19 ....30 B1
Broad La YO23 ....21 C2
Broad Oak La 18 YO32 11 A1
Broadstone Way YO30 45 A4
Broadway Gr 3 YO10 ...58 A3
Broadway YO10 ....58 A3
Broadway YO11 ....56 C1
Broadway YO10 ....57 A1
Brockfield Pk Dr YO31 47 A3
Brockfield Rd YO31 ...47 A3
Bromley St 2 YO26 ...50 B2
Brompton Rd YO30 ...45 C2
Brooklands YO10 ....53 C1
Brook St YO31 ....64 B4
Broome Cl YO32 ....42 B2
Broome Way YO32 ....42 C2
Brougham Cl YO10 ...45 A3
Broughton Way YO10 53 A1
Browney Croft YO10 ...65 C1
Brownlow St YO31 ....64 C4
Brownmoor La
Huby YO61 ....3 C3
Sutton-on-the-Forest YO61 3 C4
Brown Moor 2 YO41 ...31 A3
Brunel Ct 15 YO26 ...50 B2
Brunswick Cl 2 YO32 ...6 A1
Brunswick St YO23 ....56 A2
Buckingham St YO1 ...65 A1
Bull La Huby YO61 ....10 A4
York YO10 ....57 B4
Bull Moor La YO41 ...7 C1
Burdike Ave YO30 ....45 C1
Burdyke Inf Sch YO30 46 A1
Burlands La YO26 ....21 B4
Burlington Ave YO10 52 B1
Burnholme Ave YO31 ...53 A3
Burnholme Com Coll
YO31 ....52 C2
Burnholme Dr YO31 ...52 C2
Burnholme Gr YO31 ...52 C2
Burniston Gr YO10 ....52 C1
Burnsall Dr YO30 ....50 A1
Burns Ct YO24 ....59 A4
Burrill Ave YO30 ....46 A1
Burrill Dr 12 YO32 ...11 C3
Burton Ave YO30 ....51 A4
Burton Fields Cl 12
YO41 ....19 C3
Burton Fields Rd 4
YO41 ....19 C3
Burton Gn YO30 ....46 A1
Burton Stone La YO30 64 A4
Burtree Ave YO30 ....39 A1
Butcher Terr YO23 ...56 B2
Buttacre La YO23 ....25 C3
Buttercrambe Rd YO41 19 A4
Buttermere Dr YO30 ...45 A2
Butters Cl 20 YO32 ...10 C2
Butt Hill 3 YO19 ....23 B4
Butts Cl 7 YO41 ....19 C3
Byland Ave YO31 ....47 A1
Byron Dr YO30 ....45 B1

C

Caedmon Cl YO31 ....52 C4

Cairnborrow 4 YO24 ...59 A4
Caithness Cl 1 YO30 ...45 A4
Caldbeck Cl 1 YO30 ...45 C2
Calder Ave YO26 ....44 A1
Calf Cl YO32 ....11 A1
Calvert Cl YO10 ....41 B4
Cambrian Cl 6 YO32 ...42 B1
Cambridge St 1 YO24 55 C4
Cameron Gr YO23 ....56 B2
Campbell Ave YO24 ...55 A3
Campleshon Rd YO23 56 A2
Canal Rd YO42 ....38 B2
Canham Gr YO10 ....58 C4
Canon Lee Sch YO30 ...45 C1
Canterbury Cl 3 YO10 52 C2
Carey St YO10 ....56 C2
Carleton St 17 YO26 ...50 B2
Carlisle St 1 YO26 ...50 B2
Carl St YO23 ....56 B3
Carlton Ave YO10 ....58 A4
Carlton Rd YO41 ....31 A3
Carmelite St YO1 ....65 C2
Carmires Ave YO32 ...11 B2
Carnot St YO26 ....50 B2
Carnoustie Cl 1 YO26 49 A1
Caroline Cl 3 YO30 ...45 C2
Carrbank La YO32 ....18 A4
Carrfield YO10 ....58 B4
Carrick Gdns YO24 ...55 A3
Carr Inf Sch YO26 ....49 B2
Carrington Ave 1
YO26 ....50 A2
Carr Jun Sch YO26 ...49 B2
Carr La Escrick YO19 36 C2
Sutton-on-the-Forest YO61 4 C3
Carr Lodge YO24 ....59 A4
Carrom Cres YO24 ...59 A4
Carrs Mdw YO19 ....36 A2
Carter Ave YO31 ....52 B4
Cartman St YO10 ....56 C3
Castle Cl YO10 ....10 C2
Castlegate YO1 ....65 B2
Castle Wk YO1 ....65 B1
Cat La Bilbrough YO23 ...25 C2
Catton YO41 ....24 B4
Cavendish Gr YO10 ...15 C1
Caxton Ave YO26 ....49 C3
Cayley Cl YO30 ....45 B2
Cecilia Pl 3 YO24 ....56 A2
Cedar Glade YO19 ...23 A4
Cedar Gr YO31 ....53 A4
Cedarwood Cl 8 YO24 54 C2
Celtic Cl YO26 ....49 A2
Cemetery Rd YO10 ...65 C1
Centurion Way YO30 ...46 A4
Chaldon Cl 4 YO32 ...11 A1
Chalfonts YO10 ....58 B3
Chaloner's Cres YO24 59 C4
Chaloner's Rd YO24 ...54 B4
Chancery Ct YO24 ....54 B4
Chantry Ave 4 YO26 ...16 B2
Chantry Cl YO24 ....54 B1
Chantry Gap 1 YO26 ...16 B2
Chantry Gr 1 YO26 ...16 B2
Chantry La YO23 ....61 A1
Chapel Fields Rd YO26 54 A3
Chapel La YO23 ....26 B4
Chapel Row YO10 ....65 C1
Chapman Cl 1 YO32 ...6 B1
Chapmans Ct YO26 ...49 C3
Chapman's La YO30 ...45 C1
Chapter House St YO1 64 B3
Charles Moor YO31 ...52 B4
Charlton St YO23 ....56 B3
Chase Side Ct YO24 ...55 A1
Chatsworth Pl 18
YO32 ....42 A2
Chatsworth Terr 4
YO26 ....50 A1
Chaucer St 3 YO10 ...57 A4
Chaumont Way 1
YO32 ....42 B2
Chelkar Way YO30 ....45 B2
Chelwood Wlk 12
YO26 ....50 A1
Cherry Garth YO10 ...53 A2
Cherry Gr 8 YO26 ...16 B2
Cherry Hill La YO23 ...65 B1
Cherry La YO23 ....60 B1
Cherry Orch 7 YO32 ...11 A1
Cherry Paddock
1 Haxby YO32 ....11 A1
Kexby YO41 ....19 B3
Cherry St YO23 ....65 B1
Cherry Tree Ave
Newton-on-Derwent YO41 8 A2
York YO32 ....41 C1
Cherry Wood Cres
YO19 ....62 A2
Cheshire Ave YO32 ...41 C1
Chesney Fields 4
YO24 ....54 C2
Chessingham Gdns
YO24 ....60 A3
Chessingham Pk YO19 23 B3
Chestnut Ave YO31 ...53 B3
Chestnut Gr YO26 ....49 B1
Chestnuts The 15 YO32 11 A1

Cheviot Cl 1 YO32 ...47 B4
Chiltern Way YO32 ...42 B2
Chudleigh Rd 1 YO26 50 B2
Church Balk YO19 ....23 A4
Church Cl
Askham Bryan YO23 ...26 B4
5 Tollerton YO61 ....2 A4
Wheldrake YO19 ....37 C4
Church Farm Cl YO23 20 B3
Churchfield Dr 28
YO32 ....11 A2
Church Gn 3 YO41 ...31 B3
Church La
Appleton Roebuck YO23 33 B1
Bishopthorpe YO23 ...60 C1
Bolton Percy YO23 ....32 C1
Catton YO41 ....19 C1
Dunnington YO19 ...23 A4
4 Elvington YO41 ...31 B3
7 Haxby YO32 ....11 A2
Moor Monkton YO26 ...15 A3
Nether Poppleton YO26 44 A4
New Earswick YO32 ...42 B2
Poppleton YO26 ....16 C3
Skelton YO30 ....39 A2
10 Stamford Bridge
YO41 ....19 C3
Strensall YO32 ....11 C4
Wheldrake YO19 ....37 C4
York YO61 ....65 B2
Church Mews 2 YO26 54 B4
Church Rd
Stamford Bridge YO41 19 C3
York YO10 ....53 C1
Church Rise YO19 ...18 B2
Church St
2 Copmanthorpe YO23 26 C2
Dunnington YO19 ...23 A4
York YO61 ....65 B2
Cinder La
Upper Poppleton YO26 16 B2
Upper Poppleton YO26 16 C1
York YO31 ....52 A3
Claremont Terr YO31 ...64 B4
Clarence St YO31 ....64 B4
Claygate YO31 ....53 A3
Clay Pl 3 YO24 ....54 C2
Clementhorpe YO23 ...65 B1
Clement St 4 YO23 ...65 B1
Cleveland St YO24 ....50 C1
Cleveland Way YO32 ...42 B2
Cliffords Twr* YO1 ...65 B1
Clifford St YO1 ....65 B2
Clifton Dale YO30 ....50 C3
Clifton Moorgate YO30 46 A4
Clifton Moor Gate
YO30 ....45 A4
Clifton Pl 3 YO30 ....50 C4
Clifton Prep Sch YO30 64 A4
Clifton Rd YO30 ....64 A4
Clifton Without Jun Sch
YO30 ....45 B1
Clive Gr YO24 ....55 B3
Cloisters The YO1 ....64 C3
Cloisters Wlk YO41 ...31 B3
Close The YO10 ....45 B1
Cloverley Cl YO41 ....19 B3
Coda Ave YO23 ....27 C3
Coeside YO24 ....59 A4
Coffee Yd YO1 ....64 B3
Coggan Way YO23 ....60 B1
Coledale Cl 2 YO30 ...45 B2
Colenso St YO23 ....65 B1
Cole St YO31 ....64 B4
College of Ripon & York St
John
York YO10 ....58 A4
York YO30 ....64 A3
College Rd YO23 ....26 C3
College St YO1 ....64 B3
Colliergate YO1 ....65 B2
Collier Hag La YO23 ...25 A4
Collingwood Ave YO31 55 B3
Coll of St John The
YO31 ....64 C3
Colton Junc LS24 ....33 A4
Colton La YO23 ....33 A3
Common Croft La
YO26 ....16 A2
Common La
Dunnington YO19 ....23 B2
Sutton upon Derwent
YO41 ....31 B1
Thorganby YO19 ....38 B4
Warthill YO19 ....18 B4
York YO10 ....58 A2
Common Rd
Dunnington YO19 ...23 B4
Strensall YO60 ....6 C2
Compton St YO30 ....50 C3

Concorde Pk YO30 ....45 C4
Coneycroft 10 YO30 ....23 B4
Coneygarth La YO19 ....23 A2
Coney St YO1 ....65 B2
Conifer Cl 6 YO32 ....46 C4
Coniston Av YO10 ....45 A2
Coniston Dr YO10 ....53 A1
Connaught Way YO32 ....42 B3
Constantine Ave YO10 ....52 C1
Conway Cl 3 YO30 ....45 A4
Coombes Cl YO61 ....4 B4
Coopers Dr 4 YO23 ....26 C3
Copmanthorpe Jun Sch
YO23 ....26 C3
Copmanthorpe La
YO23 ....27 B3
Copmanthorpe Prim Sch
YO23 ....26 C3
Copmanthorpe Recn Ctr &
Sports Club YO23 ....26 C2
Copper Beeches The 2
YO19 ....23 A4
Coppergate Wlk YO1 ......65 B2
Coppergate YO1 ....65 B2
Coppice Cl 5 YO32 ....11 A2
Coppice The YO23 ....10 C1
Copwood Gr 20 YO32 ....11 B1
Corban La YO32 ....10 A3
Corban Way YO32 ....10 C2
Cornborough Av YO31 ....52 B3
Corner Cl 8 YO10 ....12 A4
Cornlands Rd YO24 ....54 A2
Cornwall Dr YO10 ....57 A1
Cornwood Way 30
YO32 ....11 A1
Cosmo Ave YO31 ....52 C2
Cotswold Way YO32 ....42 C2
Coulson Cl 7 YO32 ....6 B1
Count De Burgh Terr 4
YO23 ....56 A2
Courcey Gr YO10 ....49 B1
Courtneys YO19 ....30 C1
Courtyard The 2 YO31 ....61 A1
Covert The YO24 ....60 B4
Cowper La YO23 ....27 B1
Coxlea Gr YO31 ....53 B4
Crabtree Gr 8 YO32 ......46 C4
Cranbrook Ave YO26 ......49 B2
Cranbrook Rd YO26 ....49 B2
Cranbrooks The YO19 ....30 B1
Cranfield Pl 4 YO24 ....54 B1
Crawley Way YO31 ....53 A3
Crescent The
Kexby YO41 ....24 B2
Stamford Bridge YO41 ...19 C3
York YO24 ....65 A1
Crichton Ave YO30 ....46 A1
Crinan Ct 3 YO32 ....42 B3
Croft Ct YO23 ....60 C1
Croft Farm Cl 6 YO23 ....26 C3
Croftside 5 YO24 ....54 A4
Croftway 8 YO30 ....10 A4
Crombie Ave YO30 ....51 A4
Cromer St YO30 ....51 A4
Cromwell Rd YO1 ....65 B1
Crookland La YO32 ....11 B2
Crossfield Cres YO10 ....43 C4
Cross La Flaxton YO60 ....7 A2
Fulford YO19 ....62 B2
Crosslands Rd 2 YO32 ...46 C4
Crossmoor La YO32 ....11 A3
Cross St 5 YO24 ....54 B4
Crossways YO10 ....58 B3
Crossway The 2 YO31 ....47 A1
Crummock 3 YO32 ....59 B4
Cumberland Cl 7
YO32 ....12 A3
Cumberland St YO1 ....65 B2
Cumbrian Ave 4 YO32 ...12 A3
Cundall Cl 6 YO32 ....6 B1
Curlew Glebe 6 YO19 ....23 A4
Curzon Terr YO23 ....56 A2
Custance Wlk YO23 ....65 A1
Cycle St 4 YO10 ....57 C4
Cygnet St YO23 ....65 A1

D

Dalby Mead YO32 ....47 B2
Dale Dike Gr YO30 ....45 B3
Dale's La YO31 ....52 B3
Dale St YO23 ....65 A1
Dalguise Gr YO31 ....64 C4
Dalmally Cl YO24 ....59 A3
Dalton Hill YO19 ....10 C1
Dalton Terr YO24 ....55 C4
Dam Hill YO23 ....20 A1
Dam La YO23 ....33 B1
Dane Ave YO26 ....49 B1
Danebury Cres YO26 ......49 B1
Danebury Dr YO26 ....49 B1
Danes Croft 2 YO10 ......56 C1
Danesfort Ave YO24 ......54 A2
Danesgate YO10 ....49 B1
Danesmead YO10 ....57 C4

E

Earfit La YO23 ....26 B1
Earle St YO31 ....64 C4
Earswick Chase YO32 ....42 B4
Earswick Village YO32 ...42 B4

Daneswell Cl 3 YO41 .....19 C3
Danum Dr YO10 ....57 A1
Danum Rd YO10 ....57 A1
Darbie Cl YO32 ....41 C1
Darley Cl 7 YO41 ....19 C3
Darling La YO23 ....64 C1
Darnborough St YO23 ....65 B1
Darnbrook Wlk YO31 .....53 A2
Dauby La YO41 ....31 A4
Davygate YO1 ....65 B2
Daw La YO23 ....23 C3
Dawnay Garth YO30 ....9 A2
Daysfoot Ct 6 YO10 ......57 A4
Deacons Cl 5 YO23 ....26 C2
Dealtry Ave 8 YO32 ....11 A1
Deangate YO1 ....64 B3
Deanhead Gr YO30 ....45 A3
Deans Cl YO23 ....64 B3
Dee Cl YO24 ....59 A4
Deepdale 5 YO24 ....54 A4
Deepfurrows La YO41 ....31 C4
Deer Hill 10 YO32 ....45 A4
Deerstone Way 22
YO10 ....23 B4
De Gray Pl 5 YO23 ....27 C3
De Grey Ct YO30 ....64 A4
De Grey St YO31 ....64 B4
De Grey Terr YO31 ....64 B4
Delamere Cl 9 YO32 .....10 C2
Dell The 5 YO30 ....39 A2
Del Pyke YO31 ....64 C4
Denby Rd YO10 ....61 C4
De Mowbray Ct YO23 ....25 C4
Dennison St
YO31 ....52 A3
Dennis St YO1 ....65 C2
Deramore Dr W YO10 ....58 B4
Deramore Dr YO10 ....58 B4
Derwent Ave YO31 ....52 B1
Derwent Cl
Elvington YO41 ....31 A4
2 Stamford Bridge
YO41 ....19 C3
Derwent Ct YO41 ....31 B3
Derwent Dr YO31 ....37 B3
Derwent Est YO19 ....23 A2
Derwent Inf Sch YO10 ...53 A1
Derwent Jun Sch
YO10 ....53 A1
Derwent Rd YO19 ....30 C1
Derwent Rd YO10 ....56 C1
Deveron Way YO31 ....59 A4
Devon Pl YO10 ....56 C1
Dewsbury Terr YO1 ....64 C1
Diamond St YO10 ....64 C4
Dickens Cl 1 YO32 ....47 B2
Dickson Rd 4 YO24 ....54 B1
Dijon Ave YO10 ....55 B4
Dikelands Cl 10 YO26 ....16 B2
Dikelands La YO26 ....16 B2
Dilys Gr 5 YO26 ....50 A1
Disraeli Cl YO32 ....47 A2
Dixon La YO1 ....65 C2
Dixons Yd YO1 ....65 C2
Dodgson Terr YO26 ....49 C1
Dodsworth Ave YO31 ....52 A3
Doe Pk YO30 ....45 A4
Don Ave YO24 ....55 A1
Doriam Ave YO31 ....47 B3
Doriam Dr YO31 ....47 B3
Dovecote Garth 5
YO41 ....31 A3
Dove St YO23 ....65 B1
Dower Chase YO19 ....35 C2
Dower Pk YO19 ....36 A3
Drakes Cl YO32 ....42 C2
Drake St 2 YO23 ....65 B1
Drapers Croft
15 Copmanthorpe YO23 .26 C3
Copmanthorpe YO23 .....59 A1
Driffield Terr 2 YO24 .....56 A2
Dringfield Cl 2 YO24 .....54 C1
Dringhouses Prim Sch
YO24 ....55 B1
Dringthorpe Rd YO24 ....60 A4
Drome Rd YO23 ....27 A2
Drummond View YO23 ...61 A1
Drummond Vw 3
YO23 ....27 C3
Dudley Mews YO31 ....64 C4
Dudley St YO31 ....64 C4
Dukes Wharf YO23 ....65 B1
Duncombe La YO32 ....6 A1
Duncombe Pl YO1 ....64 B3
Dundas St YO1 ....65 C2
Dunnington C of E Prim
Sch YO19 ....23 A4
Durlston Dr YO32 ....11 B2
Dykelands Cl YO19 ....37 B4
Dykes La YO23 ....26 C2

Eason Rd YO24 ....55 A1
Eason View YO24 ....55 A1
Eastbourne Gr YO31 .....52 A3
Eastern Terr YO31 ....52 A3
Eastfield Ave YO32 ....41 B4
Eastfield Cres YO10 ......58 B3
Eastfield Ct YO10 ....58 B3
Eastfield La YO10 ....18 B1
Easthorne Dr YO10 ....45 A2
Easthorpe Dr 8 YO26 ....16 C2
East Moor Gdns YO19 ...62 B2
East Mount Rd YO24 .....56 A1
East Par YO31 ....52 A3
Eastward Ave YO10 ....62 A4
East Way YO31 ....47 A3
Eaton Ct 7 YO24 ....55 A1
Ebor Prep Sch YO30 .....55 C4
Ebor St YO23 ....65 B1
Ebor Way
7 Poppleton YO26 ....16 B2
Poppleton YO26 ....16 B2
Ebsay Dr YO30 ....45 A4
Eden Cl YO24 ....59 B4
Edgware Rd YO10 ....56 C1
Edmund Wilson Swimming
Baths YO24 ....54 C2
6 Earswick YO32 ....42 B4
York YO24 ....55 A4
Eighth Ave YO31 ....52 B2
Eldon St YO31 ....64 C4
Eldon Terr YO31 ....64 C4
Eldwick Cl YO30 ....45 B3
Elliot Ct YO10 ....64 C4
Elma Gr YO30 ....45 A3
Elm End 8 YO32 ....11 A2
Elmfield Ave YO31 ....47 B1
Elmfield Terr YO31 ....52 B4
Elm Gr YO31 ....52 B3
Elmlands Gr YO31 ....47 B1
Elmpark Vale YO31 ....47 C1
Elmpark View YO31 ....47 C1
Elmpark Way YO31 ....47 C1
Elm Tree Ave 9 YO26 ....16 B2
Elmtree Gdns 3 YO26 ...54 B4
Elston Cl YO30 ....45 C1
Elvington C of E Prim Sch
YO41 ....31 B4
Elvington La YO10 ....30 C4
Elvington La YO19 ....23 A2
Elvington Pk YO41 ....30 C4
Elvington Terr YO10 ......52 A1
Elwick Gr YO10 ....53 B1
Embleton Dr 1 YO30 .....45 B2
Emerald St YO31 ....52 A4
Emmerson St 2 YO32 ...52 C2
Enclosure Gdns 1
YO10 ....58 A2
Endfields Rd 1 YO10 .....57 A1
Enfield Cres
2 York YO24 ....55 B4
York YO24 ....55 B4
English Martyrs RC Prim
Sch YO24 ....55 B4
Ennerdale Ave YO31 .....53 A4
Escrick C of E Prim Sch
YO19 ....35 C2
Escrick Ct YO10 ....36 A2
Escrick Park Gdns
YO19 ....36 A2
Escrick St YO10 ....64 C1
Eskdale Ave YO10 ....58 B4
Esk Dr YO26 ....44 A1
Esplanade YO1 ....65 A2
Etive Pl YO1 ....59 A4
Eton Dr 2 YO32 ....10 C2
Etty Ave YO10 ....52 C1
Eva Ave YO30 ....44 C3
Evelyn Cres YO30 ....51 A4

F

Faber Cl 4 YO23 ....26 C3
Faber St YO31 ....52 A2
Fairfax Cl YO23 ....32 C1
Fairfax Croft 8 YO23 .....54 B1
Fairfax House* YO1 ......65 C2
Fairfax 15 YO41 ....19 C3
Fairfax St YO1 ....65 B1
Fairfields Dr YO30 ....39 A2
Fairway Dr 11 YO26 ......16 B2
Fairway YO31 ....45 C1
Falcon Cl 10 YO32 ....11 B2
Falconer St 1 YO24 ....55 B4
Falkland St YO1 ....65 B1
Falsgrave Cres YO30 ....51 A4
Farfield La YO19 ....18 A1
Farfield YO24 ....54 A2
Farmers Way 2 YO23 ....26 C3
Farmlands Rd 1 YO26 ...50 A1
Farmstead Rise YO32 ...41 C4
Farndale Ave YO10 ....53 C1
Farndale Cl 1 YO32 ......11 B2
Farndale St YO10 ....56 C3
Farrar St YO10 ....57 A4
Farrars Croft 16 YO23 ...54 B1
Fawcett St YO10 ....65 C1
Fawkes Dr YO24 ....49 B1
Feasegate YO1 ....65 B2
Fellbrook Ave YO26 ......49 A1

Fenwick's La YO10 ....61 C4
Fenwick St YO23 ....56 B3
Ferguson Way YO32 ......47 B2
Fern Cl YO32 ....42 C1
Fern St YO31 ....64 C4
Fernway YO10 ....58 B4
Ferry Farm Cl 2 YO19 ...27 C1
Ferry La
Bishopthorpe YO23 ......61 A1
Thorganby YO19 ....38 A2
Fetter La YO1 ....65 B2
Feversham Cres 4
YO31 ....51 B4
Fewster Way YO10 ....65 C1
Fewston Dr 9 YO30 ......45 B2
Field La YO10 ....58 B3
Field View YO31 ....52 B1
Fifth Ave YO31 ....52 B1
Filey Terr YO30 ....51 B4
Finkle St YO1 ....65 B2
Finsbury Ave YO23 ....56 B2
Finsbury St YO23 ....56 B2
Firbank Cl 3 YO10 ....11 C4
Fir Heath Cl 5 YO24 .....54 A2
Firtree Cl
8 Earswick YO32 ....42 B4
York YO24 ....55 A4
Firwood Wlk 5 YO31 .....53 B4
Fishergate Prim Sch
YO10 ....65 C1
Fishergate YO10 ....65 C1
Flavian Gr YO30 ....45 B1
Flaxman Ave YO10 ....53 C1
Flaxman Croft YO23 .....26 C3
Flaxton Rd YO32 ....12 A4
Fleet Bank La YO61 ......4 B4
Fleming Ave 8 YO31 .....52 C2
Fletcher Cl 9 YO32 ....11 A2
Fletcher's Croft 8
YO23 ....27 A3
Florence Gr YO30 ....44 C3
Folks Cl 13 YO10 ....11 C4
Fordlands Cres YO19 ....62 A2
Fordlands Rd YO19 ......62 A2
Forest Cl 9 YO32 ....47 C3
Forest Gr YO31 ....52 B3
Foresters Wlk YO41 ......19 C3
Forester's Wlk YO24 ....54 A2
Forestgate YO32 ....41 B4
Forest La YO32 ....52 B3
Forest La
Crockey Hill YO19 ....62 C1
Strensall YO32 ....41 C3
Forest of Galtres Prim Sch
YO32 ....9 B2
Forest Way YO31 ....52 A3
Forge Cl YO23 ....47 C3
Forge La YO19 ....35 C4
Foss Bank YO31 ....64 C3
Foss Ct YO31 ....47 A2
Foss Field La YO23 ......27 A1
Fossgate YO1 ....65 B2
Foss Islands Rd YO31 ...64 C3
Fossland View 4
YO32 ....11 C4
Foss Wlk YO26 ....44 A1
Foston C of E Prim Sch
YO60 ....7 A4
Foston Gr 4 YO31 ....51 B4
Fountayne St YO31 ....51 B4
Fourth Ave YO31 ....52 B1
Fox Covert YO31 ....47 B3
Foxcroft 3 YO32 ....11 A1
Fox Garth YO23 ....16 C3
Fox Glade YO41 ....19 C3
Foxthorn Paddock
YO10 ....58 C4
Foxton Cl YO24 ....54 B1
Foxwood La
3 York YO24 ....54 B1
Frances St YO10 ....56 C2
Franklins Yd YO1 ....65 C2
Fraser Ct YO30 ....45 A1
Frazer Ct YO30 ....44 C3
Frederic St YO30 ....64 A3
Friargate YO1 ....65 B2
Friars Ct YO19 ....22 C4
Friar's Wlk YO31 ....47 A1
Front St Naburn YO19 ...61 C1
York YO24 ....54 B4
Fulford Cross Spec Sch
YO10 ....56 C2
Fulford Cl YO23 ....56 C2
Fulfordgate YO10 ....56 C2
Fulford Pk YO10 ....61 C4
Fulford Rd YO10 ....56 C3
Fulford Sch YO10 ....62 C4
Furlong Rd 2 YO10 ......11 C4
Furness Dr YO30 ....45 A2
Furnwood YO31 ....53 B4
Fylingdales Ave 6
YO30 ....45 A2

G

Gable Pk YO23 ....20 B3
Gale Farm Ct 6 YO24 ....54 B4
Gale La
Thorganby YO19 ....37 B1
York YO24 ....54 B4
Gale The YO10 ....34 C1
Galligap La YO10 ....53 A1
Gallops The YO24 ....54 A1
Galmanhoe La YO1 ......64 A3
Galtres Ave YO31 ....53 A4
Galtres Gr YO30 ....50 B4
Galtres Rd YO31 ....53 A4
Ganton Pl YO24 ....59 A4
Garburn Gr YO30 ....45 A2
Garbutt Gr YO26 ....49 C2
Garbutt Way 10 YO23 ...26 C3
Gardeners Cl 20 YO23 ..26 C3
Garden Flats La YO19 ...11 B4
Garden Pl YO1 ....65 C2
Garden St YO31 ....64 B4
Garfield Terr YO26 ....50 B2
Garlands The YO30 ......45 C1
Garland St 2 YO26 ....50 A2
Garnet Terr YO26 ....50 B1
Garroway Way YO10 .....58 A1
Garrowby View 5
YO41 ....27 B3
Garrow Hill Ave YO10 ...57 C4
Garrow Hill YO10 ....57 C3
Garth Rd YO32 ....42 B1
Garths End 20 YO32 ....11 B2
Garth's End YO10 ....56 B2
Garth Terr YO30 ....51 B4
Garth View 4 YO32 ......41 C4
Gatehead La YO42 ....38 C4
Gateland Cl YO32 ....41 B4
Gay Mdws YO32 ....17 C3
Geldof Rd YO32 ....47 B2
Gennell La YO60 ....7 A4
George Cayley Dr
YO30 ....45 C4
George Ct YO31 ....64 C4
George Hudson St YO1 .65 B2
George St YO1 ....65 C2
Gerard Ave YO31 ....52 C2
Germany La YO19 ....56 C1
Giles Ave YO31 ....52 C2
Gillamoor Ave YO31 .....53 A2
Gillingwood Rd YO30 ...45 B4
Gillygate YO31 ....64 B3
Gipsey Cnr YO19 ....30 A4
Girvan Cl YO24 ....59 A4
Givendale Gr 3 YO10 ...53 B1
Glade The
Escrick YO19 ....35 C2
York YO31 ....53 A4
Gladstone St YO24 ......54 C4
Gladstone St YO31 ......64 C4
Glaisby Ct YO31 ....52 C3
Glebe Ave YO26 ....49 C2
Glebe Cl
Bolton Percy YO23 ......32 C1
3 Strensall YO32 ....12 A4
Glebe Way YO32 ....12 A2
Glen Ave YO31 ....52 A2
Glencoe St 1 YO30 ......51 A4
Glen Rd YO31 ....52 A2
Glenridding YO24 ....59 C4
Godwinsway 18 YO41 ...19 C3
Goodmanham Way YO43 52 C3
Goodwood Gr YO26 ......55 B2
Goose La YO61 ....5 C2
Goose Track La YO60 ...6 B4
Gordon St YO10 ....57 A4
Gormire Ave 8 YO31 ....47 A3
Gorse Hill 1 YO19 ....23 B4
Gorse Paddock YO32 ...47 B3
Gouthwaite Cl YO30 .....45 B3
Government House Rd
YO30 ....50 C3
Gowans The YO61 ....61 B4
Gower Rd YO24 ....45 A3
Grampian Cl 4 YO32 ....42 B2
Granary Ct YO1 ....64 B3
Grange Cl YO30 ....39 A2
Grange Garth YO10 ......56 C3
Grange La YO23 ....21 B2
Granger Ave YO26 ......49 B1
Grange St YO10 ....56 C3
Grantham Dr YO26 ......50 A1
Grants Ave YO10 ....57 A1
Granville Terr 4 YO10 ...57 A4
Grape La YO1 ....65 B2
Grasmere Dr YO10 ......53 A1
Grasmere Gr 5 YO30 ...51 B4
Grassholme YO24 ....59 B4
Grayshon Dr YO26 ......49 A2
Gray St YO23 ....65 A1
Great North Way YO26 ..44 A1
Green Acres YO32 ....42 B1
Greencliffe Dr YO30 .....50 C3
Green Cl YO30 ....45 C1
Greencroft Ct 14 YO19 ..23 B4
Greencroft La 17 YO19 ..23 B4

Green Dike 22 YO32 .....11 A1
Green Dykes La YO10 ...57 B4
Greenfield Park Dr
YO31 ....53 C4
Greengales Ct YO19 ....30 C1
Greengales La YO19 ....30 C1
Green Hills YO60 ....14 A4
Green La
Appleton Roebuck YO23 .34 A3
Bishopthorpe YO24 ......60 C3
Cottingwith YO42 ....38 B2
Wigginton YO32 ....10 C2
York YO24 ....45 C2
Green Mdws YO31 ....52 C4
Greensborough Ave 3
YO32 ....49 A2
Greenshaw Dr YO32 .....11 A3
Greenside 2 YO19 ....23 B4
Greenside 1 YO19 ....23 B4
Greenside Wlk 22
YO19 ....23 B4
Green Sward YO31 ......47 C1
Green The
22 Dunnington YO19 ...23 B4
1 Skelton YO30 ....39 A2
2 Tollerton YO61 ....54 B4
Greenway The 5 YO32 ..31 B4
Green Way YO32 ....42 B1
Greenwood Gr YO24 ....54 B1
Gregory Cl YO30 ....39 B2
Grenwich Cl 5 YO30 .....39 B2
Gresley Ct 3 YO26 ....49 A1
Grey Cl YO61 ....4 B4
Greystoke Rd YO30 ......45 A4
Grimwith Garth 8 YO30 .45 B3
Grosvenor Rd YO30 .....64 A4
Grosvenor Terr YO30 ....64 A4
Grove Gdns 12 YO26 ...16 B2
Groves La YO31 ....64 C4
Grove Terrace La
YO31 ....64 C4
Grove The YO24 ....60 B3
Grove View YO30 ....50 C3

H

Hadrian Ave YO10 ....58 A4
Hagg La Colton LS24 ....26 A1
Dunnington YO19 ....23 B3
Sutton upon Derwent
YO41 ....31 C1
Hag La YO42 ....38 B1
Haley's Terr YO31 ....46 C1
Halifax Cl 7 YO30 ....45 C2
Halifax Way YO30 ....30 C4
Halladale Cl 1 YO24 ....59 A4
Hallard Way 7 YO32 ....12 A3
Hallcroft La 8 YO23 .....26 C3
Hallfield Rd YO31 ....52 A2
Hall Pk YO10 ....58 A2
Hall Rise 12 YO32 ....12 A3
Hambleton Ave YO31 ...53 B1
Hambleton Terr YO31 ...51 B4
Hambleton View
10 Haxby YO32 ....10 C2
4 Tollerton YO61 ....54 B4
Hambleton Way YO32 ...47 B4
Hamilton Dr E YO24 .....54 C3
Hamilton Dr W YO24 ....54 C3
Hamilton Way YO24 .....55 A3
Hammerton Cl 3
YO32 ....54 B4
Hampden St YO1 ....65 B1
Handley Cl YO30 ....45 C2
Hanover St E YO26 ......50 B2
Hanover St W YO26 .....50 B2
Hansom Pl YO31 ....51 B4
Harcourt Cl
Bishopthorpe YO23 .....60 C3
Wheldrake YO19 ....37 B4
Harcourt St YO31 ....52 A2
Harden Cl YO30 ....45 B3
Hardrada Way 9 YO32 ..12 C2
Harewood Cl
Rawcliffe YO30 ....44 C3
5 Wigginton YO32 ......10 C2
Harington Ave YO10 ....52 B1
Harland Ct YO61 ....4 B4
Harlow Ct 1 YO24 ....55 B3
Harlow Rd YO24 ....55 B3
Harold Ct YO24 ....54 B1
Harolds Way 1 YO41 ....19 C3
Harrison St YO31 ....52 C3
Harrow Glade 5 YO30 ..45 B3
Hartoft St YO10 ....56 C3
Hassacarr La YO19 ......23 B3
Hastings Cl 4 YO32 .....42 C2
Hatfield Cl 8 YO30 ......45 B3
Hatters Cl 7 YO23 ....26 C3
Haughton Rd YO30 ......51 B4
Hawkshead Cl 3 YO24 ..54 A1
Hawthorne Ave 12
YO32 ....11 A2

Hawthorn Gr YO31 ....52 A2
Hawthorn Spinney
YO31 ....47 A4
Hawthorn St ■ YO31 ..52 A2
Hawthorn Terr Ctr ■
YO32 ....46 C4
Hawthorn Terr N YO32 41 C1
Hawthorn Terr S YO32 46 C4
Haxby Moor Rd YO32 ..11 B4
Haxby Rd Clifton YO31 .46 C2
New Earswick YO32 ...45 A4
York YO31 ....64 B4
Haxby Road Prim Sch
YO31 ....51 C4
Hayforth Cl YO30 ....45 C3
Hazel Cl YO32 ....46 C3
Hazel Garth YO31 ....53 A4
Hazelmere Ct YO32 ...47 A4
Hazelnut Gr YO30 ....46 A3
Hazelwood Ave YO30 .53 C1
Head Ct YO1 ....64 B3
Headland Cl ■ YO32 ..11 A2
Headlands Prim Sch
YO32 ....11 A1
Headley Cl ■ YO30 ...46 A2
Healey Gr YO31 ......47 B1
Heath Cl ■ YO32 .....55 B3
Heath Croft YO30 ....62 B4
Heather Bank
■ Stamford Bridge
YO41 ....19 C3
York YO10 ....53 B1
Heather Cl YO32 .....42 C1
Heather Croft ■ YO41 47 A3
Heathfield Rd ■ YO10 57 C4
Heath Moor Dr YO31 ..57 B1
Heath Ride YO32 .....6 A1
Hebdon Rise ■ YO25 .49 C1
Height Lands La YO23 .20 C3
Helmsdale YO24 .....59 B3
Helmsley Gr ■ YO32 ..10 C2
Hemlock Ave YO31 ...47 A2
Hempland Ave YO31 ..52 B3
Hempland Dr YO31 ...52 C4
Hempland Inf Sch
YO31 ....52 C3
Hempland Jun Sch
YO31 ....53 A3
Hempland La YO31 ...52 C4
Hendon Garth YO30 ..45 C2
Herbert St ■ YO10 ...57 A4
Herberts Way YO31 ..52 B4
Herdsman Dr ■ YO23 .27 A3
Herdsman Rd YO24 ...54 C1
Herdwick Cl ■ YO24 ..46 A2
Herman Wlk YO24 ....54 B1
Heron Ave YO31 .....54 B1
Heron Rise YO32 .....42 B2
Heslin Cl ■ YO32 ....11 A1
Heslington Croft YO10 62 B4
Heslington Ct ■ YO10 58 A2
Heslington La
Heslington YO10 ....57 C2
York YO10 ....57 A1
Heslington Prim Sch
YO10 ....58 A2
Heslington Rd YO10 ..57 A4
Hessay Pl ■ YO24 ....21 C3
Hetherton St YO30 ...64 A3
Hewley Ave YO10 ....52 C1
Heworth ARLFC YO31 .47 C1
Heworth C of E Prim Sch
YO31 ....53 B3
Heworth Gn YO31 ....64 C4
Heworth Hall Dr YO31 .52 B3
Heworth Pl YO31 .....52 B3
Heworth Rd YO31 ....52 B3
Heworth Rd YO31 ....53 C2
Heworth YO31 ....52 C3
High Catton Rd YO19 .19 C1
Highcliffe Ct YO30 ...50 C3
High Field YO10 .....18 B2
Highgrove Ct ■ YO30 .45 A4
Highlands Ave ■ YO32 12 A4
High La YO41 ....31 C4
Highmoor Cl YO24 ...54 C1
High Moor La YO30 ..2 B1
Highmoor Rd YO24 ...54 C1
High Newbiggin St
YO31 ....64 B3
High Oaks YO31 .....53 A4
High Ousegate YO1 ..65 B2
High Petergate YO1 ..64 B3
Highthorn Rd YO31 ..47 A3
Hilbeck Gr YO31 .....53 A3
Hilbra Ave YO32 .....41 C3
Hilda St ■ YO10 .....57 A4
Hillary Garth ■ YO26 .50 A1
Hillcrest Ave YO26 ...16 C2
Hill Crest Gdns YO24 .55 B2
Hill Crest YO10 .....18 B2
Hillgarth Ct ■ YO41 ..31 A3
Hillsborough Terr ■
YO30 ....51 B4
Hill St YO24 ....55 A4
Hill View YO31 .....53 B4
Hinton Ave ■ YO24 ..54 B1
Hobgate YO24 ....54 C4

Hob Moor Dr YO24 ...55 A3
Hob Moor Inf Sch
YO24 ....54 C3
Hob Moor Jun Sch
YO24 ....54 C3
Hobmoor Terr YO24 ..55 B2
Hobson Cl ■ YO23 ...26 C2
Hodgson La YO26 ....16 B1
Holburns Croft ■
YO10 ....58 A2
Holgate Bridge Gdn ■
YO24 ....54 C4
Holgate Lodge Dr
YO26 ....50 A1
Holgate Rd YO24 ....65 A1
Hollis Cres YO32 ....12 A3
Holly Bank Gr ■ YO24 55 B3
Holly Bank Rd YO24 ..55 B3
Holly Cl YO23 ....27 B1
Hollyrood Rd YO30 ..46 A3
Holly Tree Croft ■
YO19 ....23 B4
Holly Tree Garth YO32 18 A4
Holly Tree La
Dunnington YO19 ...23 B4
■ Haxby YO32 ......11 A1
Holmefield La YO10 ..57 C2
Holme Green Rd YO23 33 B1
Holme Hill La YO10 ..22 B4
Holroyd Ave YO31 ...53 B1
Holtby La YO19 .....17 C2
Homefield Cl ■ YO23 .26 C2
Homestead Cl ■ YO32 42 A4
Hope St YO10 ....65 C1
Hopgrove La N YO32 .48 B4
Hopgrove La S YO32 .48 C4
Hornby St ■ YO30 ...51 A4
Hornsey Garth ■
YO23 ....11 A2

Horseman Ave ■
YO23 ....26 C3
Horseman Cl ■ YO23 .26 C3
Horseman Dr YO23 ...26 C3
Horseman La YO23 ...26 C3
Horseshoe The YO24 .60 A4
Horsfield Way YO19 ..23 B4
Horsman Ave YO10 ..65 C1
Hospital Fields Rd
YO10 ....56 C2
Hospitum The* YO30 64 A3
Houndsway ■ YO24 ..54 A1
Howard Dr YO30 ....45 A3
Howard Link YO30 ...44 C3
Howard Rd YO32 ....12 C3
Howard St YO10 .....56 C3
Howden La YO19 ....65 C1
Howe Hill Cl YO10 ...50 A1
Howe Hill Rd YO26 ..50 A1
Howe St YO24 ....54 C4
Hubert St ■ YO23 ...55 A4
Huby Rd YO61 ......4 A4
Hudson St YO41 .....19 C3
Hudson Cres ■ YO30 50 C4
Hudson St ■ YO30 ...51 B4
Hull Rd YO10 ....22 B3
Humber Dr ■ YO32 ..12 A3
Hungate YO1 ....65 C2
Hunt Ct YO31 ....64 C3
Hunters Cl
Dunnington YO19 ...23 A4
■ Haxby YO32 ......11 A1
Hunters Way YO24 ..60 B4
Hunters Wood Way ■
YO19 ....23 A4
Huntington Prim Sch
YO32 ....42 B1
Huntington Rd YO31 .64 C4
Huntington Sch YO32 42 A1
Huntsmans La YO41 ..19 B3
Huntsman's Wlk YO24 54 A2
Hurns La YO30 ......9 C1
Hurricane Way YO30 .45 A4
Hurst's Yd YO1 .....65 C2
Hutton Cl ■ YO30 ...16 C2
Hyrst Gr YO31 ......52 A3

Ikin Way YO32 ......42 B3
Ilton Garth YO30 ....45 C3
Ingleborough Ave
YO30 ....53 A1
Ingleton Wlk ■ YO32 .12 C3
Ingram Ave YO30 ...46 B1
Ingrish La YO23 ....25 B2
Ings La
Cottingwith YO42 ...38 B2
Lillings Ambo YO60 ..6 B3
Nether Poppleton YO26 27 A3
Thorganby YO19 ....38 A2
Tollerton YO61 .....3 A4
Wheldrake YO19 ....39 A4
Intake Ave YO30 ....46 B1

Intake La
Acaster Malbis YO23 ..34 B4
Dunnington YO19 ....23 B4
Invicta Ct YO24 .....54 A1
Irwin Ave YO31 .....52 A3
Iver Cl YO26 ....49 B2

Jackson St YO31 ....64 C4
Jackson's Wlk YO23 ..25 C4
Jacobi Cl YO31 .....50 C4
James Backhouse Pl
YO31 ....55 A4
James Nicholson Way
YO30 ....46 B1
James St YO10 .....52 A1
Jamieson Terr YO23 ..56 A2
Jasmine Cl YO32 ....46 C3
Jaywick Cl ■ YO32 ..6 A1
Jedwell Cl YO32 ....41 C2
Jennifer Gr YO24 ...54 A3
Jervis Rd YO31 .....55 A1
Jewbury YO31 ......64 C3
Jockey La YO32 .....47 B3
John St YO31 ....52 A3
JORVIK –
The Viking City* YO1 65 B2
Joseph Rowntree Sch
YO32 ....42 A4
Jubbergate YO1 ....65 B2
Jubilee Terr YO26 ...50 B2
Judges Ct YO1 .....65 B2
Julia Ave YO32 .....48 A3
Juniper Cl YO32 ....46 C4
Jute Rd YO26 ....49 A2

Kathryn Ave YO32 ..47 C3
Keats Cl YO30 ......45 B1
Keble Cl ■ YO23 ...27 B3
Keble Dr ■ YO23 ...27 C3
Keble Gdns ■ YO23 .27 C3
Keble Park Cres ■
YO23 ....27 C3
Keble Pk N YO23 ...27 C3
Keble Pk S YO23 ...27 C3
Keepers Way ■ YO19 23 B4
Keith Ave YO32 .....42 C1
Keldale ■ YO32 ....11 B2
Kempton Cl ■ YO24 .54 C2
Kendal Cl ■ YO32 ...23 B4
Kendrew Cl ■ YO24 ..54 A1
Kenlay Cl YO32 .....41 C1
Kennedy Dr ■ YO32 .41 A2
Kenrick Pl ■ YO26 ..49 A2
Kensal Rise YO10 ...54 B3
Kensington Ct ■ YO24 55 B1
Kensington Rd YO24 .54 B1
Kensington St YO23 ..56 A2
Kentmere Dr YO30 ..45 B2
Kent St YO10 ....65 C1
Kerver La YO19 ....23 B4
Kestrel Wood Way
YO31 ....47 B3
Keswick Way ■ YO30 54 A3
Kexby Ave YO10 ...54 C3
Kexby Bridge* YO41 .24 B3
Kexby House* YO41 ..24 B3
Kexby Stray YO41 ...23 C2
Key Way YO10 .....62 B2
Kilburn Rd YO10 ...55 A4
Kimberlows Wood Hill ■
YO10 ....58 B4
Kinbrace Dr YO30 ...59 A4
Kings Acre YO31 ....53 A3
Kingsclere YO32 ....42 B2
Kingsland Terr ■
YO26 ....50 B2
Kings Moor Rd YO32 .17 C4
King's Sq YO1 ......65 C2
Kings Staith YO1 ...65 B2
King St YO1 ....65 B2
Kingsway Jun Sch
YO24 ....54 A4
Kingsway N YO30 ...51 A1
Kingsway W YO24 ...54 A4
Kingswood Gr YO24 .54 C2
Kir Cres YO24 ......54 B4
Kirk Balk La YO60 ..1 A4
Kirkcroft ■ YO32 ...11 A1
Kirkdale Rd YO10 ...53 C1
Kirkham Ave ■ YO31 .53 A4
Kirklands YO32 .....12 A3
Kirkstone Dr YO30 ..50 C2
Kirk View ■ YO24 ...54 A3
Kirkwell YO23 .....60 C1
Kitchener St YO31 ...51 C4
Kitemere Pl ■ YO30 .59 A4
Kitty Garth YO19 ...37 C4
Knapton Cl ■ YO30 .44 C3
Knapton La YO26 ...49 A1
Knavesmire Cres YO23 56 A2

Knavesmire Prim Sch
YO23 ....56 A2
Knavesmire Rd YO23 55 C2
Knoll The YO24 .....54 A3
Kyle Cl ■ YO61 .....2 A4
Kyle Way YO32 .....44 A1
Kyme St YO1 ....65 B1

Laburnum Cl YO31 ...20 B3
Laburnum Garth ■
YO31 ....52 A2
Laburnum Gr YO19 ..34 C1
Lady Hamilton Gdns
YO30 ....45 C2
Lady Pecketts Yd YO1 65 C2
Lady Rd YO32 ......51 A4
Ladysmith Mews ■
YO32 ....11 C4
Lakeside YO10 .....34 B4
Lakeside Dr YO30 ...45 A3
Lakeside Prim Sch
YO30 ....45 B3
Lambert Ct YO1 ....64 B2
Lamel St YO10 .....57 C4
Lamplugh Cr ■ YO23 27 C3
Lancar Cl ■ YO32 ...10 C2
Landau Cl YO30 ....45 B1
Landing La
■ Haxby YO32 ......11 B2
York YO26 ....50 A3
Landings The ■ YO32 11 B2
Lane The YO41 .....19 A3
Langdale Ave YO31 ..54 B3
Langholme Dr YO26 .49 B3
Langley Ct ■ YO32 ..42 A4
Lang Rd
Bishopthorpe YO23 ..60 B1
York YO26 ....42 B3
Langrickgate La YO42 38 B4
Langsett Gr YO30 ...58 B4
Langton Ct ■ YO23 ..11 C3
Langwith Stray YO10 29 B3
Lansdowne Terr ■
YO23 ....56 A2
Lansdown Way ■
YO32 ....11 B2
Lanshaw Croft YO30 .45 B2
Larchfield YO31 ....47 B3
Larchfield Cl ■ YO23 .26 C3
Lavender Gr YO24 ...50 A2
Laveracks Ind Est
YO41 ....31 A4
Lawnswood Dr YO30 .45 B1
Lawnway YO31 .....52 C4
Lawrence St YO10 ...57 A4
Lawson Rd YO24 ...60 A4
Layerthorpe YO31 ..64 C3
Leadley Croft ■ YO23 26 C1
Lead Mill La YO1 ...65 C1
Leake St YO10 .....57 A4
Lea Way YO32 .....42 C1
Leeman Rd YO26 ...65 A2
Leeside YO24 ......55 A1
Leicester Way YO1 ..65 C1
Leighton Croft ■
YO30 ....45 B2
Lendal YO1 ....65 B2
Lerecroft Rd YO24 ..54 C1
Lesley Ave YO10 ...57 A1
Leven Rd YO24 ....59 C4
Levisham St YO10 ..56 C3
Leyes The YO10 ....53 B1
Leyfield Cl ■ YO32 ..11 A2
Leyland Rd YO31 ...53 C2
Lichfield Ct ■ YO23 .56 A2
Lidgett Grove Sch
YO26 ....49 A3
Lidgett Gr YO26 ...49 A3
Lilac Ave
Appleton Roebuck YO23 33 B2
York YO10 ....57 B1
Lilac Gr YO32 ......41 C1
Lilbourne Dr YO30 ..45 C1
Lilling Ave ■ YO31 ..47 A1
Lilling La YO60 .....1 A4
Lilling Low La YO60 ..6 B3
Lime Ave YO31 ....54 B4
Limegarth ■ YO26 ..16 B2
Lime Tree Ave YO32 46 C4
Lime Tree Mews ■
YO19 ....23 B4
Lincoln St ■ YO26 ..51 B2
Lindale ■ YO24 ....59 B4
Linden Cl YO32 ....42 B2
Lindel St ■ YO31 ...55 B4
Lindley Wood Gr YO30 45 A1
Lindsey Ave YO26 ..49 C1
Lingcroft La YO19 ..28 B3
Link Ave YO30 .....46 B1

Link Rd YO31 ......47 A3
Link The
■ Copmanthorpe YO23 .26 C3
York YO10 ....57 A1
Linnet Way YO24 ...54 B1
Linton Rd ■ YO26 ..16 C2
Linton St ■ YO26 ..51 B2
Lister Way YO30 ...50 C4
Little Ave YO30 ....46 A1
Littlefield Cl ■ YO26 ..54 C3
Little Garth ■ YO26 ..16 C2
Little Hallfield Rd
YO31 ....52 A2
Little La ■ YO32 ....11 A1
Little Mdws ■ YO32 .11 A1
Little Stonegate YO1 .65 B3
Livingstone St ■ YO23 55 C2
Lloyd Cl YO10 .....57 A1
Lob La YO41 ....19 C3
Lochrin Pl ■ YO26 ..49 A1
Lockey Croft ■ YO32 11 A2
Lockwood St YO31 ..64 C4
Lofthouse La YO41 ..24 C4
Long Close La YO10 ..57 A4
Longcroft ■ YO32 ..11 A2
Longfield Terr YO30 ..64 A3
Long Furrow ■ YO32 11 A2
Long La Catton YO41 .24 C3
Grimston YO19 ....29 B4
Long Ridge Dr ■
YO30 ....45 A4
Long Ridge La YO26 .16 C2
Longwood Link ■
YO30 ....45 A4
Longwood Rd YO30 ..45 A4
Lord Mayor's Wlk
YO31 ....64 B3
Lords Moor La YO32 .12 B4
Loriners Dr ■ YO23 ..26 C3
Lorne St YO23 .....56 A3
Lorraine Ave ■ YO24 31 A3
Love La York YO10 ..57 A2
Low Catton Rd YO41 .19 B2
Low Croft ■ YO32 ...11 A2
Lower Darnborough St
YO23 ....65 B1
Lower Friargate YO1 .65 B2
Lower Priory St YO1 .65 A1
Loweswater Rd ■
YO30 ....45 A2
Low Farm Cl YO23 ..32 C1
Lowfield Dr YO32 ...42 A3
Low Field La YO23 ..21 B3
Lowfield La YO26 ...21 C3
Lowfield Rd ■ YO24 ..54 B1
Low Fields Dr YO24 ..54 B1
Low Gn YO23 ......26 C2
Lowick YO24 ......59 A4
Low La YO23 ......54 C4
Low Mill YO41 ....58 C4
Low Moor Ave ■ YO10 57 B1
Low Moor La
Askham Richard YO23 25 B4
Hessay YO26 ......15 B1
Lown Hill YO24 ....54 B2
Low Ousegate YO1 ..65 B2
Low Petergate YO1 ..65 B3
Low Poppleton La
YO26 ....49 A4
Lowther Ct ■ YO31 ..51 C4
Lowther St YO31 ...64 C4
Lowther Terr YO24 ..55 A4
Low Well Pk YO19 ..37 B4
Low Westfield Rd
Askham Bryan YO23 .26 B2
Copmanthorpe YO23 .26 B2
Loxley Cl YO30 ....45 B3
Lucas Ave YO30 ...46 B2
Lucombe Way YO32 .41 C2
Lumley Rd YO30 ...51 A4
Lund Cl ■ YO22 ...11 A1
Lundgreen La YO61 ..3 C4
Lundy Cl ■ YO30 ...59 A4
Lycett Rd YO23 ....60 B3
Lydham Ct ■ YO24 ..54 B1
Lyndale Ave YO10 ..58 B4
Lynden Way YO24 ..54 B4
Lynwood Ave ■ YO26 26 C3
Lynwood View ■
YO23 ....26 C3
Lysander Cl ■ YO30 .45 C4

Main St continued
Escrick YO19 ......36 A2
Hessay YO26 ......15 A1
■ Naburn YO19 ....27 C1
Poppleton YO26 ...16 B2
Shipton YO30 .....9 B2
Stamford Bridge YO41 19 C3
Wheldrake YO19 ...37 B4
York YO10 ....56 C1
York YO30 ....58 A2
York YO26 ....21 C4
Malbys Gr ■ YO23 ..26 C2
Malham Gr YO31 ...53 A2
Mallard Way ■ YO24 54 B1
Mallory Cl YO32 ...41 C1
Malt Kiln La YO23 ..33 B2
Malton Ave YO31 ...52 A3
Malton La YO60 ...7 C2
Malton Rd
Huntington YO32 ..47 C2
York YO31 ....52 B4
Malton Way YO30 ..51 A4
Malt Shovel Ct YO1 .65 C2
Malvern Ave YO26 ..49 C2
Malvern Cl YO32 ...42 C2
Mancroft YO32 .....11 A1
Manley Cl YO32 ...41 C1
Manor Beeches The ■
YO19 ....23 A4
Manor C of E Sch
YO23 ....49 B4
Manor Ct YO23 ....42 B3
Manor Dr ■ YO19 ..23 A4
Manor Dr N YO26 ..49 C1
Manor Dr S YO26 ..49 C1
Manor Farm Cl ■
YO23 ....26 C2
Manor Garth YO32 ..10 C1
Manor Heath YO23 ..26 C3
Manor La YO30 ....44 C3
Manor Park Cl YO30 .45 A3
Manor Park Gr YO30 45 A3
Manor Park Rd YO30 45 A3
Manor Way YO30 ...45 A3
Mansfield St YO31 ..64 C3
Maple Ave YO23 ...27 C3
Maple Ct YO10 ....62 B3
Maple Gr YO10 ....56 C2
Maplewood Paddock ■
YO24 ....54 B2
March St YO31 ....64 C4
Margaret St YO10 ..65 C1
Market St YO1 .....65 B2
Markham Cres YO31 .64 B4
Markham St YO31 ..64 B4
Marlborough Cl YO30 45 A2
Marlborough Gr YO10 56 C3
Marmiam Dr ■ YO32 17 C3
Marston Ave YO26 ..54 A4
Marston Cres YO26 .54 A4
Marston La YO26 ...54 A4
Marten Cl ■ YO30 ..45 C1
Martin Cheeseman Ct ■
YO24 ....54 B1
Marygate La YO30 ..64 A4
Marygate YO30 ....64 A4
Mask La YO41 .....24 C1
Mattison Way YO24 .55 A1
Mayfield Gr YO24 ..55 A1
Maypole Gr ■ YO19 .27 C1
Maythorn Rd YO31 ..47 A3
Maythorpe YO23 ...20 B3
Meadlands YO31 ...53 A3
Meadowbeck Cl YO10 53 A1
Meadow Cl ■ YO23 .55 A1
Meadowfields Dr YO31 46 C3
Meadow La YO19 ...11 A1
Meadows The ■ YO30 39 A2
Meadow Way
York YO26 ....52 B4
York YO32 ....42 B1
Melander Cl YO26 ..49 A1
Melander Gdns ■
YO32 ....41 C4
Melbourne St YO10 .56 C3
Melcombe Ave ■
YO31 ....11 C4
Melrose Cl ■ YO31 ..52 C2
Melrosegate YO31 ..52 B2
Melrose's Yd YO1 ..65 C2
Melton Ave YO30 ...45 B1
Melton Dr
■ Bishopthorpe YO23 ..27 C3
York YO30 ....45 B1
Melwood Gr YO26 ..49 A2
Mendip Cl ■ YO32 ..42 B2
Merchant Adventurers
Hall*
YO1 ....65 C2
Merchantgate YO1 ..65 C2
Merchant Taylors Hall*
YO31 ....64 C3
Merchant Way YO23 .26 C3
Merlin Covert ■ YO31 47 B4
Metcalfe La YO31 ...53 B2

Micklegate Bar Mus★
  YO24 ....65 A1
Micklegate YO1 ....65 A2
Middle Banks **24** YO32 .11 A2
Middlecroft Dr YO32 ...11 C4
Middlecroft Gr **2**
  YO32 ....12 A4
Middleham Ave YO31 .47 A1
Middlethorpe Dr YO24 60 A4
Middlethorpe Gr YO24 60 B4
Middleton Rd 54 B3
Middlewood Cl YO23 ..20 B3
Midgley Cl **5** YO41 ...19 C3
Midway Ave **5** 16 C2
Mildred Gr **8** YO24 ...55 B3
Milestone Ave YO23 ...20 B3
Milford Mews **7** YO32 41 C4
Milford Way YO32 ......41 C4
Millers Croft **12** YO23 .26 C3
Millfield Ave YO10 .....57 B4
Millfield Gdns YO26 ...16 C2
Millfield La
  Nether Poppleton YO26 .44 A1
  Poppleton YO26 ....16 C2
  York YO10 ....57 C4
Millfield Rd YO23 ......56 A3
Millgates YO26 ....49 B3
Mill Hill Dr YO32 ....42 B1
Mill Hill YO19 ....36 A2
Mill La
  Acaster Malbis YO23 ..27 B1
  Askham Bryan YO23 ...26 B3
  Askham Richard YO23 .25 C3
  Haxby YO32 ....10 C2
  Hessay YO23 ....20 A4
  York YO10 ....52 A3
Mill Mount Ct YO24 ...55 C4
Mill Mount YO24 ....55 C4
Mill St YO1 ....65 C1
Millthorpe Sch YO23 ..56 A3
Milner St YO24 ....54 C4
Milson Gr YO10 ....57 C4
Milton Carr **8** YO30 ..45 B2
Milton Gr YO10 ....57 B4
Minchin Cl **3** YO30 ...46 A2
Minster Ave YO31 ......47 B3
Minster Cl **3** YO32 ...11 A1
Minster Sch The YO1 .64 B3
Minster View **2** YO32 .11 A1
Minster Yd YO1 ....64 B3
Minster Cl **2** YO24 ...54 A2
Mistral Ct YO31 ....47 A1
Mitchell La YO41 ....19 C1
Mitchell's La YO41 .....57 B1
Miterdale **4** YO24 ....59 B4
Moat Field YO10 ....53 B1
Moatside Ct YO31 ......64 B3
Moiser Cl YO32 ....41 C1
Monk Ave YO31 ....52 B4
Monk Bar Ct YO31 .....64 B3
Monkbridge Ct YO31 ..64 C4
Monkgate Cloisters
  YO31 ....64 C3
Monkgate YO31 ....64 C3
Monks Cross Dr YO32 .47 C4
Monks Cross Link
  YO32 ....43 A1
Monkton Rd
  York YO31 ....47 A1
  5 York YO31 ....47 B2
Montague Rd **14** YO23 .27 C3
Montague St YO23 .....56 B2
Montague Wlk **6**
  YO26 ....16 B2
Montrose Ave YO31 ...46 C1
Moor Cl **1** YO19 ......30 B1
Moorcroft Rd YO24 ...59 C4
Moore Ave YO31 ....53 A1
Moorgarth Ave
  10 York YO24 ....55 B3
  3 York YO24 ....55 C3
Moorgate YO24 ....54 C4
Moor Gr YO24 ....55 A1
Moor La
  Bishopthorpe YO23 ....27 B2
  Catterton LS24 ....25 A2
  Copmanthorpe YO23 ..26 C2
  Earswick YO32 ....11 C2
  Haxby YO32 ....10 C4
  Knapton YO26 ....21 B4
  Murton YO19 ....17 C1
  Naburn YO19 ....27 C1
Moorland Garth **2**
  YO32 ....11 C4
Moorland Rd YO10 ....56 C1
Moorlands La
  Skelton YO30 ....39 B3
  1 Tollerton YO61 .....2 A4
Moor La
  Newton-on-Ouse YO30 ..8 B4
  Rufforth YO23 ....21 A3
  Skelton YO30 ....39 C3
  Strensall YO32 ....12 A4
  Thornton-le-Clay YO60 ..14 A2
  York YO24 ....59 B3

Moor Rd YO41 ....19 C3
Moor Way YO32 ....42 C1
Morehall Cl YO30 ......45 B3
Morritt Cl YO31 ....47 B1
Moss St YO24 ....65 A1
Mount Ephraim **6**
  YO24 ....55 C4
Mount Par YO24 ....55 C4
Mount Sch The YO24 .55 C4
Mount The YO24 ....65 A1
Mount Vale Dr YO24 ..55 C3
Mount Vale YO24 ......55 C3
Mowbray Dr YO26 .....49 B1
Muirfield Way **6** YO26 49 A2
Mulberry Ct YO32 .....42 B3
Mulberry Dr **7** YO32 .11 A2
Mulwith Cl YO31 ......52 C3
Muncastergate YO31 .52 A4
Murray St YO24 ....55 B4
Murrough Wilson Pl **3**
  YO31 ....51 B4
Murton Garth YO19 ...22 B4
Murton La YO19 ....22 C4
Murton Way YO19 .....22 B4
Museum St YO1 ....65 B2
Myrtle Ave YO23 ......27 C3

N
Naburn La
  Deighton YO19 ....35 C4
  Fulford YO19 ....61 C1
Naburn Park Mews
  YO19 ....28 A1
Nairn Cl YO24 ....59 B3
Nalton Cl **9** YO23 ....26 C2
Narrow La YO42 ....38 C4
National Centre for Early
  Music★ YO1 ....65 C2
National Rly Mus★
  YO26 ....50 C1
Navigation Rd YO1 ....65 C2
Nelson's La YO24 .....55 B2
Nelson St YO31 ....64 C4
Nessgate YO1 ....65 B2
Nether Way YO26 ......16 B2
Netherwindings **10**
  YO32 ....11 B2
Netherwoods **5** YO32 .11 B2
Neville Dr **8** YO23 ...27 C3
Neville St YO31 ....64 C4
Neville Terr YO31 ......64 C4
Nevinson Gr YO10 ....57 A1
Nevis Way YO24 ....59 A4
Newborough St YO30 .64 A4
Newbury Ave YO24 ...54 C2
Newby Terr YO31 ......51 B4
Newdale **3** YO32 ....11 B2
New Earswick Prim Sch
  YO32 ....41 C1
New Forge Ct **11** YO32 11 B2
Newgate Ct YO1 ....65 B2
Newgate YO1 ....65 B2
New La
  Bishopthorpe YO23 ....60 C1
  Huntington YO32 ......47 C2
  Lillings Ambo YO60 ....5 A4
  Long Marston YO23 ...25 A4
Newland Park Cl YO10 57 C4
Newland Park Dr YO10 57 B4
Newlands Dr YO26 ....49 A3
Newlands La YO26 ....16 A1
Newlands Rd YO23 ....60 B1
New La Strensall YO32 ..6 A1
Nidd Cl YO26 ....49 A4
Nidd Dr YO26 ....49 A4
Nidd Gr YO24 ....55 A1
Nigel Gr **7** YO24 .....55 C3
Nightingale Cl YO32 ..47 A2
Ninth Ave YO31 ....52 B2
Norfolk St YO23 ....56 B3
Norman Dr YO26 ......49 A3
Norman St **5** YO10 ..57 A4
Norseway YO41 ....19 C2
Northcote Ave YO24 ..54 B4
Northcroft **8** YO32 ..11 B2
North Field Ave YO23 .33 B2
North Field Cl YO23 ..33 B2
North Field La
  Askham Bryan YO23 ..33 B2
  Upper Poppleton YO26 ..21 B4
Northfield Sch YO26 ..49 A2
Northfields **5** YO32 ..6 A1

North Field Way YO23 .33 B2
Northgate La YO41 ....18 C3
North La YO32 ....43 C2
Northlands Ave **1**
  YO32 ....42 B4
North La
  Wheldrake YO19 ....37 B4
  York YO24 ....55 C1
  York YO32 ....43 B4
Northminster Bsns Pk
  YO26 ....21 B4
North Moor Gdns
  YO32 ....42 B2
North Moor Rd YO32 .42 B2
North Moor **7** YO32 .42 B2
Northolme Dr YO30 ..45 A2
North Par YO30 ....44 A3
North St YO1 ....65 B1
Norway Dr YO10 ....56 C1
Nunnill St YO23 ....56 B3
Nun Monkton Prim Sch
  YO26 ....9 C2
Nunnery La YO23 .....65 B1
Nunthorpe Ave YO23 .56 A3
Nunthorpe Cres YO23 .56 A2
Nunthorpe Gr YO23 ..56 A3
Nunthorpe Rd YO23 ..65 A1
Nursery Cl YO26 ....16 C2
Nursery Dr YO24 ......55 A4
Nursery Gdns YO10 ..58 B4
Nurseru Rd **4** YO26 .16 C2

O
Oak Busk La YO60 .....7 B2
Oakdale Rd YO30 ......45 B3
Oaken Grove Sch YO32 41 A1
Oak Glade **8** YO31 ..47 B4
Oakhill Cres YO32 .....11 C3
Oakland Ave YO31 ....52 C4
Oakland Dr YO31 ......52 C4
Oaklands Sch YO24 ...54 B3
Oaklands Sports Ctr
  YO24 ....54 B3
Oaklands **6** YO32 ....12 A4
Oak Rise **7** YO26 ....54 B4
Oak St **3** YO26 ....50 A2
Oak Tree Cl YO32 .....12 A4
Oak Tree Gr YO32 .....12 A4
Oak Tree La YO32 .....41 B4
Oak Tree Way **16** YO32 12 A4
Ogleforth Mews YO1 ..64 B3
Ogleforth YO1 ....64 B3
Old Coppice **2** YO32 .11 B2
Old Dike Lands **34**
  ....11 A1
Old Hall La YO41 ......24 B2
Old Lane Ct LS24 .....33 A4
Old Moor La YO24 ....60 A4
Old Orch YO32 ....11 A1
Old Orch The
  Fulford YO10 ....62 A4
  Shipton YO30 ....9 B2
Old Rd YO32 ....33 A2
Old St The LS24 ....25 B1
Old Village The YO32 .42 B2
Orchard Cl
  Appleton Roebuck YO23 .33 B2
  York YO24 ....55 A2
Orchard Cotts **41** YO23 23 B4
Orchard Gdns YO31 ..47 A3
Orchard Paddock
  6 Haxby YO32 ....11 A1
  34 Haxby YO32 ....11 A2
Orchard Rd **7** YO26 ..16 C2
Orchard View YO30 ...39 A2
Orchard Way
  1 Strensall YO32 .....12 A4
  York YO32 ....55 A2
Ordnance La YO10 ....56 C2
Oriel Gr YO10 ....45 C1
Orrin Cl YO24 ....59 B4
Osbaldwick La YO10 ..53 A1
Osbaldwick Link Rd
  YO10 ....53 C1
Osbaldwick Prim Sch
  YO10 ....53 B1
Osbaldwick Village
  YO10 ....53 B1
Osbourne Dr **4** YO24 .45 A4
Osmington Cl **3**
  YO23 ....11 C4
Osprey Cl **2** YO24 ...54 A1
Ostler's Cl **8** YO23 ...27 A3
Osman Rd YO30 ....49 B2
Otterwood Bank **6**
  YO24 ....54 A2
Otterwood La YO24 ...54 A2
Otterwood Paddock
  YO41 ....19 B3
Our Ladys RC Prim Sch
  YO24 ....55 A2
Ouse Acres YO26 ......49 C3
Ousebuern Ave YO26 .49 B3
Ousecliffe Gdns YO30 .50 C1
Outgang La YO19 .....53 C3
Overdale Cl YO24 .....54 A4
Overton Rd YO30 .....16 B4

Ovington Terr YO23 ...56 A3
Owlwood Ct **7** YO19 .23 A4
Owlwood La **8** YO19 .23 A4
Owston Ave YO10 .....57 C4
Ox Calder Cl **16** YO19 .23 B4
Ox Carr La YO32 ....11 B2
Ox Cl YO41 ....19 C3
Oxford St **5** YO24 ...55 C4

P
Paddock Cl **13** YO23 .26 C2
Paddock The YO26 ....49 B3
Paddock Way YO26 ...49 B3
Palmer La YO1 ....65 C2
Palmes Cl YO19 ....28 A1
Panman La YO19 ......18 B1
Parade Ct YO31 ....52 B3
Paragon St YO1 ....65 C1
Park Ave YO32 ....41 C2
Park Cres YO31 ....64 C4
Parker Ave YO26 ......54 A3
Park Gate YO32 ....6 A1
Park Grove Sch YO31 .64 C4
Parkland Way **5** YO32 11 A1
Park La YO24 ....55 B4
Parkside Cl YO24 .....55 A4
Park St **5** YO23 .....65 A1
Park St YO24 ....65 A1
Parliament St YO1 ....65 B2
Parsons La YO10 ......16 A2
Paston Wlk YO31 .....65 B1
Pasture Cl
  Skelton YO30 ....39 A2
  2 Strensall YO32 .....12 A3
Pasture Farm Cl YO10 .61 C1
Pasture La YO31 ......47 B3
Pastures The **4** YO24 .55 A1
Pately Pl **1** YO26 ....49 C1
Patrick Pool YO1 ......65 B2
Patterdale Dr YO10 ...45 A2
Pavement YO1 ....65 B2
Paver La YO1 ....65 C2
Pear Tree Ave **8** YO26 .36 A2
Pear Tree Cl YO32 ....42 B1
Peartree Ct YO1 ......64 C3
Peasholme Gn YO1 ...65 C2
Peckitt St YO1 ....65 B1
Peel Cl YO10 ....57 C2
Peel St YO23 ....56 B1
Pembroke St YO30 ...44 A4
Penley's Grove St
  YO31 ....64 C4
Pennine Cl YO32 ......42 B1
Penny La Ct YO1 ......64 C4
Pentland Dr YO32 ....47 A4
Penyghent Ave YO31 .51 C4
Peppercorn Cl **6**
  YO26 ....50 A1
Percy's La YO1 ....65 C2
Percy St YO31 ....64 B4
Petercroft Cl **5** YO19 .23 B4
Petergate YO1 ....64 B3
Peter Hill Dr YO30 ...51 A4
Peter La YO1 ....65 B2
Petersway YO30 ......64 A4
Pheasant Dr **5** YO24 .54 A1
Philadelphia Terr **2**
  YO23 ....56 A3
Piccadilly YO1 ....65 C2
Pike Hills Mount YO23 .26 C3
Pilgrim St YO31 ....64 B4
Pinelands **6** YO31 ...50 A1
Pinelands Way YO10 ..58 B4
Pinewood Gr **8** YO31 .47 A3
Pinewood Hill **4** YO10 58 B4
Pinfold Ct **4** YO30 ..50 C4
Plantation Cl YO26 ...49 B3
Plantation Dr YO26 ..49 B3
Plantation Way **22**
  YO32 ....11 A2
Ploughlands **1** YO32 .11 C4
Ploughman's Cl **4**
  YO23 ....27 A3
Ploughman's La YO32 .41 B4
Plumer Ave YO31 .....51 C2
Pollard Cl YO32 ....47 A4
Poplar Gr YO32 ....42 A1
Poplar St **5** YO26 ...50 B1
Poppleton Hall Gdn
  YO26 ....16 C3
Poppleton Rd YO26 ..50 A1
Poppleton Road Prim Sch
  YO26 ....50 B1
Poppleton Sta YO26 ..16 B2
Portisham Pl **12** YO10 11 C4
Portland St YO31 .....64 B4
Postern Cl YO23 ......65 A1
Postern Cl YO23 ......65 A1
Pottery La **19** YO31 ..52 A4
Pottery Dr **22** YO31 ..52 A4
Pottery La **7** YO31 ...52 A4
Precentor's Ct YO31 ..64 B3
Prestwick Ct YO30 ...49 A2
Price's La YO23 ....65 B1
Priest La YO19 ....23 B2

Princess Rd YO32 .....12 A4
Prior's Wlk YO26 .....49 C2
Priory St YO1 ....65 A1
Priory Wood Way
  YO31 ....47 B3
Prospect Terr
  Fulford YO10 ....61 C3
  York YO1 ....65 B1
Pulleyn Cl **3** YO32 ..46 B1
Pulleyn Dr YO24 ......55 B2
Purey Cust Nuffield Hospl
  The YO31 ....64 B3

Q
Quaker Gn **1** YO24 ..59 B4
Quant Mews YO10 ...58 A4
Queen Anne's Rd YO30 64 A3
Queen Margarets Sch
  YO19 ....35 C2
Queen's Staith Rd YO1 65 B2
Queen St YO24 ....65 A1
Queenswood Gr YO24 54 C3
Queen Victoria St
  YO23 ....56 A2

R
Racecourse Rd YO23 .56 A1
Railway Terr YO24 ....50 C1
Rainsborough Way **3**
  YO30 ....45 C1
Raker Cl YO19 ....37 B4
Ralph Butterfield Sch
  YO32 ....11 B2
Rampart The YO32 ...11 B2
Ramsay Cl YO31 ......64 C4
Ramsey Ave YO23 ....56 A2
Ratcliffe Ct YO30 .....39 B2
Ratcliffe St YO30 .....51 A4
Raven Gr YO26 ....54 A4
Rawcliffe Ave YO30 ..45 B1
Rawcliffe Cl YO30 ....45 B2
Rawcliffe Croft YO30 .44 C2
Rawcliffe Dr YO30 ...45 A2
Rawcliffe Inf Sch YO30 45 A2
Rawcliffe La YO30 ....45 B2
Rawcliffe Way YO30 ..45 A2
Rawdon Ave YO10 ...52 B1
Ray Dike Cl YO32 .....42 B1
Rectory Cl YO23 ......32 C1
Rectory Gdns YO23 ..56 A2
Redcap La YO42 ......38 B2
Redcoat W **1** YO31 ..11 C4
Redeness St YO31 ....52 A3
Redhill Field La YO23 .25 C2
Red House Prep Sch
  YO26 ....15 C4
Redman Cl YO10 ......56 B1
Redmayne Sq YO32 ..6 A1
Redmires Cl YO30 ....45 C3
Redthorn Dr YO31 ...47 B2
Red Twr★ YO1 ....52 A1
Redwood Dr **6** YO32 .11 A2
Reeves The YO24 .....54 B2
Regency Mews **2**
  YO24 ....55 B1
Regents Ct **14** YO26 .50 B2
Regent St YO10 ......57 A4
Reginald Gr YO23 ....56 B3
Reighton Ave YO30 ..45 B1
Reighton Dr **10** YO30 .45 B1
Renshaw Gdns **6**
  YO26 ....50 A1
Retreat Hospl The
  YO10 ....57 B3
Reygate Gr **3** YO23 ..26 C1
Ribstone Gr YO31 ....53 A3
Rice La YO60 ....7 B3
Richard III Mus★ YO1 64 B3
Richardson St YO23 ..56 B3
Richmond St YO31 ...52 A2
Ridgeway YO26 ....54 A4
Ringstone Rd YO30 ..45 B4
Ripley Gr **8** YO30 ...45 B1
Risewood YO41 ....19 A3
Rishworth Gr YO30 ..45 B3
Rivelin Way YO30 ....45 B3
Riversdale **12** YO41 ..11 B2
Riverside Cl **1** YO41 .31 B3
Riverside Cres YO23 .42 B3
Riverside Gdns
  8 Elvington YO41 .....31 B3
  2 Poppleton YO26 ...16 B2
Riverside Wlk
  1 Poppleton YO26 ...16 B2
  5 Strensall YO32 .....11 C4
River St YO23 ....65 B1
Riversvale Dr **21** YO32 6 A1
Robert Wilkinson Prim Sch
  YO32 ....6 A1
Robin Gr **8** YO24 ...55 B4
Robinson Dr YO24 ...54 A3
Roche Ave YO31 ......47 A1
Rockingham Ave YO31 52 C2
Rolston Ave **3** YO30 .44 C1
Roman Ave N **17** YO41 19 C3
Roman Ave S YO41 ...19 C2

Ropers Ct **2** YO23 ...27 A3
Ropewalk The YO31 ..52 A2
Roseberry Gr YO30 ..45 B4
Roseberry St YO26 ...50 B3
Rosecomb Way **6**
  YO32 ....41 C4
Rosecroft Way YO30 .45 A1
Rosedale Ave YO26 ..49 B1
Rosedale St YO10 ....56 C3
Rosemary Ct YO1 ....65 C2
Rosemary Pl YO1 .....65 C2
Rose La YO32 ....51 B4
Rose Tree Gr YO32 ...41 C1
Rosslyn St **1** YO30 ..50 C3
Rougier St YO1 ....65 A2
Round Hill Link YO30 .45 B3
Rowan Ave YO32 .....41 C1
Rowan Pl YO32 ....41 C1
Rowley Ct **2** YO32 ..42 B4
Rowntree The YO30 ..39 B1
Rowntree Ave YO30 ..46 B1
Royal Chase YO24 ...55 B1
Royal Dragoon Guard
  Association Regimental
  Mus★ YO1 ....65 B2
Ruby St **3** YO23 .....56 A2
Rudcarr La YO19 ......18 A2
Ruddings Cl **12** YO32 .11 A1
Ruddings YO10 ....30 C1
Ruffhams Cl YO19 ...30 B1
Rufforth Prim Sch
  YO23 ....20 B3
Runswick Ave YO26 ..49 A1
Rushwood Cl **6** YO32 .11 B2
Russell St YO23 ......56 A3
Russet Dr YO31 ......53 A2
Rutland Cl **7** YO23 ..26 C3
Ryburn Cl YO30 ......45 B3
Rydal Ave YO31 ......52 C3
Rye Cl **11** YO32 .....11 A1
Ryecroft Ave YO24 ..59 B4
Ryecroft Cl YO31 .....48 B1
Ryecroft **8** YO32 ....47 C2
Ryehill Cl YO32 ....41 C2
Ryemoor Rd **20** YO32 .11 A1
Rylatt Pl YO24 ....54 A4

S
Sadberge Ct YO10 ....58 B4
Saddlers Cl
  18 Copmanthorpe YO23 .26 C3
  Huntington YO32 ......47 B3
Sails Dr YO24 ....58 A4
St Aelreds Cl YO31 ...52 B1
St Aubyn's Cl YO24 ..55 C3
St Barnabas Ct **2**
  YO24 ....50 B2
St Benedict Rd YO23 .65 A1
St Catherines Cl YO30 .39 B2
St Chads Wharf YO23 .56 B1
St Clement's Gr YO23 .56 B3
St Denys' Rd YO1 ....65 C2
St Edward's Cl YO24 .55 B1
St Andrewgate YO1 ..65 B2
St Andrew Pl YO1 ....65 C2
St Andrews Ct YO1 ...65 C3
St George's RC Prim Sch
  YO10 ....56 C3
St Giles Ct YO31 .....64 B3
St Giles Rd YO30 .....39 A2
St Giles Way YO23 ...26 C2
St Helen's Rd **6** YO24 .55 A1
St Helen's Rise YO19 .37 C4
St Helen's Sq YO1 ...65 B2
St James Cl YO30 ....45 A4
St James Mount YO24 55 C3
St James Pl **5** YO24 .54 A1
St John's Cres YO31 .64 C4
St John's Rd **8** YO41 .19 C3
St John St YO31 ......64 B3
St Lawrences Ct Prim
  Sch YO10 ....57 A4
St Leonard's Pl YO1 ..64 B3
St Luke's Gr YO30 ....51 A4
St Margaret's Terr
  YO1 ....52 A1
St Mark's Gr YO30 ...45 A3
St Martin's La YO1 ...65 A2
St Marys Cl YO42 ....38 B2
St Marys C of E Prim Sch
  YO23 ....25 C4
St Marys Cl YO10 ....53 B1
St Mary's Terr YO30 ..64 A3
St Mary's YO30 ....64 A3
St Matthew's Cl **4**
  YO19 ....27 C1
St Maurice's Rd YO31 64 C3
St Nicholas Cl **3** YO26 .26 C3
St Nicholas Cres **2**
  YO23 ....26 C3
St Nicholas Croft YO23 26 A4
St Nicholas Pl **1** YO10 57 B4

St Nicholas Rd 3
YO23 . . . . .26 C3
St Nicholas Way 22
YO32 . . . . .11 A2
St Olave's Rd 64 A4
St Olave's Sch YO30 . . . .64 A4
St Oswalds C of E Prim Sch
YO10 . . . . .62 A4
St Oswald's Rd YO10 . .56 C1
St Pauls Mews 54 C4
St Paul's Sq YO24 . . . . . .55 C4
St Paul's Terr YO24 . . . . .21 C4
St Peters Cl YO30 . . . . . .21 C4
St Peter's Gr YO30 . . . . .64 A4
St Peters Sch YO30 . . . .64 A4
St Philip's Gr YO30 . . . . .45 B1
St Sampsons Sq YO1 . .65 B2
St Saviourgate YO1 . . . .65 C2
St Saviour's Pl YO1 . . . .65 C2
St Stephen's Rd YO24 .54 B3
St Stephen's Sq YO24 .54 B3
St Swithin's Wlk YO26 .50 A1
St Thomas' Pl YO24 2
St Thomas's Cl 2
YO31 . . . . .53 B1
St Wilfrids Cl 7 YO32 12 A3
St Wilfrid's Rd 6 YO32 12 A3
St Williams Coll YO31 .64 B3
St Wulstan Cl YO31 . . . .52 A4
Salisbury Rd YO26 . . . . .54 B3
Salmond Rd 8 YO24 . .54 A2
Sampson Ct YO24 . . . . . .49 C2
Sandacre Ct YO26 . . . . .49 C2
Sandcroft Cl 4 YO26 . . .54 C4
Sandcroft Rd YO24 . . . .54 C4
Sandhill La YO41 . . . . . . .31 C3
Sandholme 2 YO32 . . . .11 B2
Sand Hutton C of E Prim
Sch .14 A2
Sand Hutton Ct YO41 . .14 A2
Sandmartin Ct YO24 . . .54 C1
Sandown Cl YO24 . . . . . .55 A3
Sandringham Cl YO24 .41 B4
Sandringham St YO10 .56 C4
Sandstock Rd YO31 . . . .53 A4
Sandy Gap YO10 . . . . . . .41 B4
Sandy La 12 YO22 . . . . . .11 A2
Sandyland 2 YO32 . . . . .11 A2
Sandy La YO32 . . . . .13 A1
Sandyridge 9 YO26 . . . .16 C2
Sargent Ave YO23 . . . . . .60 B1
Saville Gr YO23 . . . . .45 C1
Sawyer's Cres 20 YO23 26 C3
Sawyers Wlk 9 YO23 23 B4
Saxon Way 8 YO32 . . . .10 C2
Saxon Cl YO30 . . . . .9 B2
Saxon Pl YO31 . . . . .52 A4
Saxon Rd YO24 . . . . .19 C3
Saxon Vale YO30 . . . . . . .9 B2
Scafell Cl 4 YO30 . . . . .45 A2
Scaife Gdns YO31 . . . . . .51 B4
Scaife St YO31 . . . . .51 B4
Scarborough Terr
YO30 . . . . .64 A4
Scarcroft Hill YO24 . . . .56 A3
Scarcroft La YO23 . . . . . .65 A1
Scarcroft Prim Sch
YO23 . . . . .65 A1
Scarcroft Rd YO24 . . . . .65 A1
Scaudercroft 13 YO19 23 B4
Scawton Ave 11 YO31 .47 C3
School Cl 18 YO10 . . . . .19 C3
School La YO30 . . . . .54 C1
Askham Richard YO23 . . .25 C4
Bishopthorpe YO23 . . . . . . .60 C1
18 Copmanthorpe YO23 . .26 C2
Poppleton YO26 . . . . .16 B2
York YO10 . . . . .58 A2
School St YO24 . . . . .62 A4
Scoreby La YO41 . . . . . . .19 A2
Scotchman La YO60 . . . .7 C1
Scott Moncrieff Rd
YO32 . . . . .12 A3
Scott St YO23 . . . . .56 B3
Scriven Gr 6 YO32 . . . . .11 B2
Scrope Ave 4 YO31 . . . .52 A2
Seafire Cl 6 YO30 . . . . . .12 A3
Seakel La YO23 . . . . .28 B3
Seaton Cl YO10 . . . . .53 B1
Second Ave YO31 . . . . . .52 B3
Sefton Ave YO31 . . . . . . .47 B1
Segrave Wlk 10 YO26 .50 A1
Selby Rd YO19 . . . . .62 A3
Seldon Rd YO26 . . . . . . .50 A2
Seventh Ave YO31 . . . . .52 B2
Severn Gr YO26 . . . . .44 B1
Severus Ave YO26 . . . . .49 C1
Severus St YO24 . . . . . . .54 C4
Seymour Gr YO31 . . . . . .52 B3
Shallowdale Gr 1
YO10 . . . . .58 A3
Shambles YO1 . . . . .65 B2
Shaw's Terr YO24 . . . . . .65 A1
Shelley Gr YO30 . . . . . . .45 B2
Sherringham Dr YO24 .54 C1

Sherwood Gr
Huntington YO32 . . . . . . .47 B2
York YO26 . . . . .49 A3
Shilton Garth Cl 3
YO32 . . . . .42 B4
Shipton Low Rd YO30 . . .9 A2
Shipton Rd
Clifton YO30 . . . . .45 B1
Rawcliffe YO30 . . . . .44 C3
York YO30 . . . . .50 C4
Shipton St 3 YO30 . . . . .51 A4
Shirbutt La YO19 . . . . . . .15 B1
Shirley Ave YO26 . . . . . .49 B3
Shotel Cl YO10 . . . . .45 B1
Sills La YO30 . . . . .16 C3
Silverdale Ct YO24 . . . . .59 C4
Silver St YO1 . . . . .65 B2
Sim Balk La YO24 . . . . . .60 A2
Sirocco Ct YO31 . . . . . . .46 C1
Sitwell Gr YO26 . . . . .49 B2
Siward St YO10 . . . . .57 C4
Sixth Ave YO31 . . . . .52 A2
Skates La YO61 . . . . .4 A4
Skeldergate YO1 . . . . . . .65 B2
Skelton Ct 3 YO30 . . . . .50 C3
Skelton Prim Sch
YO30 . . . . .39 B2
Skewsby Gr YO31 . . . . . .47 B2
Skiddaw YO24 . . . . .59 B4
Skipwith Rd YO19 . . . . . .36 A3
Slessor Rd YO24 . . . . . . .54 A2
Slingsby Gr YO24 . . . . . .55 A1
Smales' St YO1 . . . . .65 B1
Smary La YO19 . . . . .22 C4
Smeaton Gr YO26 . . . . . .49 B2
Smeaton Rd YO41 . . . . . .24 C4
Smith Cl YO10 . . . . .57 B1
Smithie Cl YO32 . . . . .41 C2
Smith's La YO60 . . . . .6 C2
Snowdon Cl YO23 . . . . . .25 C4
Somerset Ct 6 YO30 . . .45 A4
Somerset Rd YO41 . . . . .46 C1
South Back La YO61 . . . .2 A3
South Bank Ave 2 YO23 56 A2
South Down Rd 3
YO23 . . . . .42 B2
Southfield Cres 2
YO24 . . . . .55 A1
Southfields Rd YO32 . . .12 A4
Southlands 4 YO32 . . . .11 A2
Southlands YO23 . . . . . . .56 A3
Southlands Rd YO23 . . .56 A3
Southolme 7 YO30 . . . .44 C3
Southolme Dr 7 YO30 45 B2
South Par YO24 . . . . .65 A1
South Ruddings La
YO19 . . . . .37 B4
Southwood Rd YO41 . . .31 B1
Sowerby Rd YO26 . . . . . .49 C1
Spalding Ave YO30 . . . . .51 A4
Speculation St YO1 . . . . .65 C2
Spencer St 3 YO23 . . . .65 B1
Speng La YO26 . . . . .20 A1
Spen La YO1 . . . . .64 C3
Spey Bank YO24 . . . . . . .59 B3
Spindle Cl YO24 . . . . .54 B1
Springbank Ave YO10 .60 B4
Springbank Gr YO19 .23 A4
Springfield Cl 6 YO32 .53 B4
Springfield Rd 4 YO26 16 B2
Springfield Way YO26 .49 A3
Spring La YO19 . . . . .57 C2
Springwood YO32 . . . . . .41 C4
Spruce Cl YO7 . . . . .46 C3
Spurriergate YO1 . . . . . .65 B2
Stabler Cl 15 YO32 . . . . .10 C2
Stablers Wlk YO32 . . . . .42 B4
St Aelreds RC Prim Sch
YO31 . . . . .52 B2
Staindale Cl 3 YO30 . . .45 A3
Staithes Cl 4 YO26 . . . . .4 B1
Stamford Bridge Prim & Inf
Sch YO41 . . . . .19 C3
Stamford Bridge Rd
YO19 . . . . .18 B3
Stamford Bridge W
YO41 . . . . .19 B3
Stamford St E 16 YO26 .50 B2
Stamford St W 8
YO26 . . . . .50 B2
Stanley Ave YO32 . . . . . .41 C4
Stanley St YO31 . . . . .64 C4
Starkey Cres YO31 . . . . .52 C2
Station Ave York YO1 . . .65 A2
Station La YO19 . . . . .46 C4
Station Rd
Copmanthorpe YO23 . . . .26 C2
Haxby YO32 . . . . .11 B2
Poppleton YO26 . . . . .16 B1
2 Poppleton YO26 . . . . . .16 B2
Tollerton YO61 . . . . .2 A4
York YO1 . . . . .65 A2
Station Rise 4 YO1 . . . .65 A2
Station Sq 4 YO24 . . . . .12 A4

Steeple Cl 4 YO32 . . . . .10 C2
Steeton La LS24 . . . . .32 C4
Stephenson St YO41 . . .47 A2
Stephenson Way YO26 .50 B2
Sterne Ave YO31 . . . . . . .52 C2
Sterne Way YO61 . . . . . . .4 A4
Stewart La YO19 . . . . .34 B1
Stirling Gr YO10 . . . . .57 B1
Stirling Rd YO30 . . . . .54 B1
Stirrup Cl YO24 . . . . .54 A1
Stockhill Cl 1 YO19 . . .23 A4
Stockholm Cl 1 YO10 .56 C1
Stockton La
Heworth YO32 . . . . .48 C2
York YO31 . . . . .54 B2
Stockton on the Forest City
Prim Sch YO32 . . . . .17 C4
Stonebow The YO1 . . . . .65 C2
Stonegate Arc YO1 . . . .64 B3
Stonegate YO1 . . . . .64 B3
Stonelands Ct 2 YO30 45 C2
Stone Riggs YO32 . . . . . .17 C4
Stonethwaite 5 YO24 .59 B4
Stoop Cl 2 YO32 . . . . . . .11 A1
Stow Ct YO32 . . . . .47 A4
St Pauls C of E Prim Sch
YO24 . . . . .55 B4
Straight La YO19 . . . . . . .18 B1
Stratford Way YO41 . . . . .19 A3
Stray Garth YO31 . . . . . . .52 B4
Straylands Gr YO31 . . . .47 B1
Stray Rd YO31 . . . . .53 A3
Street La LS24 . . . . .32 C4
Strensall Pk YO32 . . . . . .11 C2
Strensall Rd
Earswick YO32 . . . . .42 C4
York YO32 . . . . .42 B3
Stripe La YO30 . . . . .39 A2
Stuart Cl 4 YO32 . . . . . . .42 B4
Stuart Rd YO24 . . . . .54 C2
Stubden Gr YO30 . . . . . . .45 B3
Sturdee Gr YO31 . . . . . . .51 C4
Summerfield Rd YO24 .56 A1
Sunningdale Cl 1
YO24 . . . . .49 A2
Sunnydale 3 YO24 . . . . .41 C4
Surrey Way YO30 . . . . . . .45 B3
Surtees St YO30 . . . . .51 A4
Sussex Cl YO10 . . . . .45 B2
Sussex Rd YO10 . . . . .45 B2
Sussex St 14 YO32 . . . . .11 C4
Sutherland St YO23 . . . .56 A2
Sutor Cl 17 YO23 . . . . . .26 C3
Sutton Bridge★ YO41 .31 B3
Sutton on Derwent C of E
Prim Sch YO41 . . . . .31 B3
Sutton-on-the-Forest C of
E Prim Sch YO61 . . . . .1 B1
Sutton Way YO30 . . . . . .44 C3
Swale Ave YO24 . . . . .55 A1
Swan Cl YO19 . . . . .35 C4
Swan Farm Ct YO19 . . . .35 C4
Swann St YO23 . . . . .65 A1
Swinegate YO1 . . . . .65 B2
Swinsty Ct YO30 . . . . . . .45 B2
Sycamore Ave YO32 . . .41 C1
Sycamore Cl
1 Haxby YO32 . . . . .41 C4
Skelton YO30 . . . . .39 B2
Sycamore Pl YO30 . . . . . .64 A3
Sycamore Terr YO30 . . .64 A3
Sycamore View 17
YO26 . . . . .16 B2
Sykes La YO61 . . . . .2 A4

T

Tadcaster Rd YO24 . . . . .55 C2
Tadcaster Road
Dringhouses YO23 . . . . . . .60 A2
York YO24 . . . . .55 C2
Tang Hall La YO31 . . . . .52 C2
Tang Hall Prim Sch
YO31 . . . . .52 B2
Tanner Row YO1 . . . . . . .65 A2
Tanner's Moat YO1 . . . . .65 A2
Tarbert Cres 2 YO24 . . .59 A4
Tatton Cl YO30 . . . . .45 C2
Teal Dr YO24 . . . . .54 B1
Tedder Rd YO24 . . . . .54 A2
Telford Terr 1 YO24 . . . .56 C3
Temple Ave YO10 . . . . . .53 A1
Temple Garth YO23 . . . .27 A2
Temple La YO23 . . . . .27 A2
Templemead YO31 . . . . .52 A4
Temple Rd YO23 . . . . . . .60 B1
Tennent Rd YO24 . . . . . .54 A1
Tennyson Ave YO30 . . . .51 B4
Ten Thorn La YO23 . . . . .21 C3
Terry Ave YO1 . . . . .65 B1
Terry St YO23 . . . . .56 B3
Thanet Rd YO24 . . . . .54 B1
Thatchers Croft 31
YO23 . . . . .26 C3
Theresa Cl 13 YO31 . . .47 B2
Thief La YO10 . . . . .57 B2
Third Ave YO31 . . . . .52 B2
Thirkleby Way YO10 . . . .53 B1

Thirlmere Dr YO31 . . . . .52 C3
Thomas St 2 YO10 . . . . .57 A4
Thompson Dr YO41 . . . . .6 A1
Thompson Pl 6 YO26 . .50 A2
Thoresby Rd YO24 . . . . .54 A2
Thorncroft YO19 . . . . . . .23 B4
Thornfield Ave 5
YO31 . . . . .47 B1
Thornfield Dr 2 YO31 .47 A3
Thornhills 18 YO32 . . . .11 B2
Thorn Nook YO31 . . . . . .47 B1
Thornton Moor Cl 6
YO24 . . . . .54 B2
Thornwood Covert 1
YO24 . . . . .54 B2
Thorpe St YO23 . . . . .56 A3
Tilmire Cl 3 YO10 . . . . . .57 B1
Timber Cl YO32 . . . . .20 C3
Tisbury Rd YO26 . . . . . . .50 A1
Tithe Cl YO24 . . . . .54 B1
Toby Ct YO32 . . . . .11 C4
Toft Gn YO1 . . . . .65 A2
Tollerton Rd YO30 . . . . . .8 A4
Top La YO23 . . . . .26 C3
Toremill Cl YO32 . . . . . . .41 C1
Torridon Pl YO24 . . . . . . .59 A4
Tostig Ave YO26 . . . . . . .49 B2
Tostig Cl 14 YO41 . . . . . .19 C3
Tower St YO1 . . . . .65 B1
Town End Gdns 3
YO32 . . . . .10 C2
Townend St YO31 . . . . . .64 B4
Towthorpe Moor La
YO32 . . . . .12 B2
Towthorpe Rd YO32 . . . .11 B2
Towton Ave
9 York YO24 . . . . .55 B3
1 York YO24 . . . . .55 C3
Trafalgar St YO23 . . . . . .56 B3
Tranby Ave YO10 . . . . . . .53 C1
Trenchard Rd YO26 . . . .49 A3
Trent Ave 4 YO32 . . . . . .42 B3
Trentholme Dr 2
YO24 . . . . .55 C3
Trent Way YO24 . . . . .59 C4
Trevor Gr 8 YO24 . . . . . .55 B3
Trinity La YO1 . . . . .65 A2
Troon Cl 2 YO26 . . . . . . .49 A2
Troutbeck 7 YO24 . . . . .59 B4
Troutsdale Ave YO30 . . .44 C3
Tudor Rd YO24 . . . . .54 B3
Tudor Way YO32 . . . . .6 B1
Tuke Ave YO10 . . . . .53 A1
Turnberry Dr YO26 . . . . .49 A1
Turner's Croft YO10 . . . .57 C2
Turnmire Rd 4 YO24 . . .55 B2
Twin Pike Way 14
YO32 . . . . .10 C2
Tyn Garth YO19 . . . . .27 C1

U

Ullswater YO24 . . . . .59 C4
Undercroft 7 YO19 . . . . .23 A4
Union Terr YO31 . . . . .64 B4
University of York
Heslington YO10 . . . . .57 B2
York YO10 . . . . .57 A4
York YO10 . . . . .58 A3
York YO10 . . . . .64 A3
University Rd YO10 . . . . .57 B3
Uppercroft 8 YO32 . . . .11 A1
Upper Hanover St 8
YO26 . . . . .50 B2
Upper Newborough St 1
YO30 . . . . .51 B4
Upper Poppleton Jun Sch
YO26 . . . . .16 B2
Upper Price St YO23 . . .56 B3
Upper St Paul's Terr
YO24 . . . . .50 C1
Usher La YO32 . . . . .11 B3

V

Vale The YO30 . . . . .39 A2
Valley View YO31 . . . . . . .37 B4
Vanbrugh Dr YO10 . . . . .58 B4
Vavasour Ct 16 YO23 . . .26 C2
Vernon Cl 8 YO23 . . . . . .27 C3
Vernon Rd YO31 . . . . . . .45 A3
Vesper Dr YO24 . . . . .54 A4
Vesper Wlk YO32 . . . . . .42 B3
Vicarage Gdns 1
YO10 . . . . .53 B1
Vicarage La YO19 . . . . . .28 A1
Vicars Cl 5 YO23 . . . . . . .26 C2
Victoria Ct YO26 . . . . . . .50 B2
Victoria Farm Cl YO23 20 B3
Victoria St 1 YO23 . . . . .65 B1
Victoria Way YO32 . . . . .47 B1
Viking Cl 20 YO19 . . . . . .19 C3
Viking Rd
Stamford Bridge YO41 . . . .19 C3
York YO26 . . . . .49 B2
Village Garth 1 YO32 . .11 A2
Village St YO30 . . . . .45 A4

Village The
Haxby YO32 . . . . .11 A2
Skelton YO30 . . . . .39 A2
Stockton on the Forest
YO32 . . . . .17 C4
Stensall YO32 . . . . .12 A4
Villa Gr 2 YO31 . . . . .52 A3
Vincent Way YO24 . . . . .54 B1
Vine St YO23 . . . . .56 B3
Vyner St YO31 . . . . .51 B4

W

Waggoners Dr 20
YO23 . . . . .26 C3
Waincroft 3 YO32 . . . . . .11 C3
Wains Cl 21 YO23 . . . . . .26 C2
Wains Gr YO24 . . . . .59 C4
Wain's Rd YO24 . . . . .54 C1
Walker Dr YO24 . . . . .54 B1
Walker La YO41 . . . . .37 B4
Walkington La YO30 . . . .2 A1
Walmgate YO1 . . . . .65 C2
Walney Rd YO31 . . . . . . .52 C2
Walnut Cl YO10 . . . . .60 B4
Walpole St YO31 . . . . . . .51 C4
Walton Pl YO26 . . . . .54 A4
Walworth St N 4
YO26 . . . . .50 A2
Walworth St S 10 YO26 50 B2
Wandhill 11 YO32 . . . . . .11 A1
Wandle The YO26 . . . . . .21 C2
Wansbeck 8 YO24 . . . . .59 A4
Ward Ct YO23 . . . . .65 B1
Warehill La YO61 . . . . .2 B3
Warthill C of E Prim Sch
YO19 . . . . .14 B3
Warwick St YO31 . . . . . . .51 C4
Wasdale Cl 2 YO30 . . . .45 A2
Waterdale Pk YO31 . . . . .47 A2
Water End YO26 . . . . .50 A2
Waterings 18 YO32 . . . . .10 C2
Water La
6 Clifton YO30 . . . . .45 C2
Dunnington YO19 . . . . .23 C4
York YO30 . . . . .50 C4
Waterman Ct 3 YO24 .54 A2
Water World★
YO31 . . . . .47 C3
Wath La YO41 . . . . .19 B1
Watson St YO24 . . . . .56 B3
Watson Terr 2 YO24 . . .56 B3
Wattlers Cl 3 YO23 . . . .27 A3
Waveney Gr YO30 . . . . . .46 A1
Waverley St YO31 . . . . . .64 C4
Waynefleet Gr 1 YO10 57 C4
Weavers Cl 11 YO23 . . .26 C2
Weddall Cl YO24 . . . . . . .55 B2
Welborn Cl YO10 . . . . . . .57 C4
Welland Rise YO26 . . . . .49 C2
Wellesley Cl YO31 . . . . . .47 C4
Wellington Row YO1 . . .65 A2
Wellington St YO10 . . . .57 A4
Weiton Ave YO26 . . . . . . .49 C2
Welwyn Dr YO10 . . . . . . .57 A1
Wenham Rd YO24 . . . . . .54 B1
Wenlock Dr YO19 . . . . . .36 A3
Wenlock Terr YO10 . . . . .56 C3
Wensleydale Dr YO10 . .53 C1
Wentworth Rd YO24 . . .54 A4
Werkdyke The YO1 . . . . .64 C3
Wesley Pl YO1 . . . . .65 C2
West Bank YO24 . . . . . . .55 A4
West Moor La YO23 . . . .33 B2
West End Cl 9 YO32 . . . .12 A4
West End YO19 . . . . .11 C4
Westerdale Ct 2 YO30 50 C3
Westfield Cl YO32 . . . . . .11 A2
Westfield Cty Inf Sch
YO24 . . . . .54 A3
Westfield Cty Jun Sch
YO26 . . . .
Westfield Dr YO10 . . . . . .56 C1
Westfield Gr 12 YO32 . . .10 C2
Westfield La YO19 . . . . . .37 C2
Westfield Pl
18 Haxby YO32 . . . . .11 A2
York YO24 . . . . .21 C2
Westfield Rd 20 YO32 . .11 A2
Westholme Gr YO41 . . . .46 C1
Westlands Gr YO31 . . . . .52 B4
Westminster Rd YO30 . .50 C2
West Moor La YO41 . . . .58 A1
Westpit La YO32 . . . . .42 B4
West Thorpe YO24 . . . . .54 A3
Westview Cl YO26 . . . . . .49 A4
West Vwood La YO32 . . .21 A1
Westwood Mews 12
YO19 . . . . .23 B4
Westwood Terr YO23 . . .56 A2
Wetherby Rd YO26 . . . . .54 B4
Wharfe Dr YO24 . . . . .54 C1
Wharncliffe Dr YO30 . . .45 B3
Wharton Ave YO31 . . . . .52 C4
Wharton Rd 8 YO41 . . . .19 C3
Wheatcroft 6 YO32 . . . .11 B3
Wheatfield La YO32 . . . .11 A1

Wheatlands Gr YO26 . . .49 B3
Wheatley Dr 17 YO32 . .11 A1
Wheelhouse The 4
YO30 . . . . .39 A2
Wheelwright Cl
2 Copmanthorpe YO23 .26 C3
Sutton upon Derwent
YO41 . . . . .31 B2
Wheldrake C of E Prim Sch
YO19 . . . . .38 B4
Wheldrake Ings Nature
Reserve★ YO19 . . . . .38 B4
Wheldrake La
Crockey Hill YO19 . . . . .29 A2
Escrick YO19 . . . . .36 A2
Whenby Gr YO31 . . . . . . .47 B2
Whernside Ave YO31 . . .52 C2
Whin Cl
3 Strensall YO32 . . . . . . .12 A3
York YO24 . . . . .60 B4
Whinfield Ave YO31 . . . .60 B4
Whinny La YO60 . . . . . . .13 C4
Whin Rd YO24 . . . . .60 B3
Whip-ma-whop-ma-gate
YO1 . . . . .65 C2
Whitby Ave YO31 . . . . . . .52 C4
Whitby Dr YO31 . . . . .52 C4
White Cross Rd YO31 . .51 C4
White Horse Cl 8
YO32 . . . . .42 B2
White House Dale
YO24 . . . . .55 B2
White House Dr YO24 . .55 B2
White House Gdns 4
YO24 . . . . .55 C3
White House Rise
YO24 . . . . .55 B2
White Rose Ave 3
YO32 . . . . .46 C4
White Rose Cl YO26 . . . .44 B2
Whiterose Dr YO41 . . . . .19 C3
White Rose Gr 9
YO32 . . . . .46 C4
White Rose Way YO26 .44 B1
Whitestone Dr YO31 . . .47 A3
Whitethorn Cl YO31 . . . .47 A3
Whitley Cl YO30 . . . . .54 A1
Whitley Rd YO41 . . . . . . .30 C4
Whitton Pl YO10 . . . . . . .53 B1
Wigginton Prim Sch
YO32 . . . . .10 C2
Wigginton Rd YO31 . . . .64 B4
Wigginton Terr YO31 . . .46 B1
Wilberforce Ave YO30 . .51 A4
Wilkinson Way 3
YO32 . . . . .11 C4
William Plows Ave
YO10 . . . . .57 A3
Willis St YO10 . . . . .57 A4
Willoughby Way YO24 . .54 A1
Willow Bank YO12 . . . . .42 A1
Willow Ct YO41 . . . . .19 B3
Willow Glade YO32 . . . . .47 B4
Willow Gr
Earswick YO32 . . . . .42 C4
York YO31 . . . . .52 B4
Willows The 8 YO32 . . . .12 A4
Wilsthorpe Gr 4 YO10 .57 C4
Wilstrop Farm Rd 11
YO23 . . . . .26 C2
Wilton Rise YO24 . . . . . . .55 B4
Wimpole Cl 8 YO30 . . . .45 C2
Winchester Ave 3
YO26 . . . . .50 A1
Winchester Gr 1
YO26 . . . . .50 A1
Windermere YO24 . . . . . .59 C4
Windmill La YO10 . . . . . .58 A3
Windmill Rise YO26 . . . .55 A4
Windsor Dr 2 YO32 . . . .10 C2
Windsor Garth YO24 . . .54 C2
Winscar Gr 12 YO30 . . . .45 A4
Winterscale St YO10 . . .56 C3
Wisker La YO32 . . . . .43 B4
Witham Dr YO32 . . . . . . .42 C3
Woldcroft YO41 . . . . .31 B3
Wolfe Ave YO31 . . . . .52 B2
Wolsey Dr 6 YO23 . . . . .27 C3
Wolsley St YO10 . . . . . . .57 A4
Wolviston Ave YO10 . . . .58 A4
Wood Cl 8 YO32 . . . . . . .11 C4
Woodcock Cl 6 YO32 . .11 B2
Woodford Pl 1 YO24 . . .54 C2
Woodhouse Gr
YO31 . . . . .52 C4
Woodland Chase YO30 46 A2
Woodland Pl YO32 . . . . .42 A1
Woodlands Ave YO8 . . . . .
Woodlands YO31 . . . . . . .11 A1
Woodlands Gr YO31 . . . .36 A2
Woodlands Gr YO31 . . . .52 C4
Woodland Way YO32 . . .42 B1

72 Woo – Yor

Woodlea Ave YO26 .....49 B1
Woodlea Bank YO26 ...49 C1
Woodlea Cres YO26 ...49 C1
Woodlea Gr YO26 ......49 C2
Woodleigh Cl ① YO32 .11 C3
Woodside Ave YO31 ...52 C3
Wood St YO31 ....52 A3
Woodthorpe Prim Sch
YO24 ....59 B4
Wood Way YO32 ......42 C1

Woolnough Ave YO10 .58 A4
Worcester Dr YO31 ...53 A2
Wordsworth Cres
YO24 ....59 C4
Wray's Ave YO31 .....47 A2
Wycliffe Ave YO10 ...58 A4
Wydale Rd YO10 ......53 C1

Y

Yarburgh Gr ② YO26 .50 A2
Yarburgh Way YO10 .58 B4
Yearsley Cres YO31 ...51 C4

Yearsley Grove Jun Sch
YO32 ....47 B2
Yearsley Gr YO31 .....47 A2
Yearsley Swimming Baths
YO31 ....46 C1
Yew Tree Cl
Acaster Malbis YO23 ...27 B1
Rufforth YO23 ....20 B3
Yew Tree Mews YO19 .53 B2
York Abbey★ YO1 ...64 A3
York Bridge Rd YO61 ...2 A3
York Castle Mus★ YO1 65 C1

York City Art Gall★
YO30 ....64 B3
York City Football Club
YO30 ....64 A4
York Coll of Further &
Higher Ed YO24 .....60 A3
York Cricket & RUFC
YO30 ....50 B4
York District Hospl
YO30 ....64 B4
York Dungeon★ YO1 .65 B2
York La YO60 ....7 A1
York Minster★ YO1 ...64 B3

York Race Course (The
Knavesmire)★ YO24 .55 C2
York Rd
Bilbrough YO23 ......25 A3
Dunnington YO19 ....22 C3
Haxby YO32 ....41 C4
Naburn YO19 ....27 C1
Stillingfleet YO19 ....34 C1
Strensall YO32 ......11 C3
Sutton-on-the-Forest YO61 4 B1
Sutton-on-the-Forest YO61 4 B3
York YO26 ....54 B4

York Rugby League Club
YO32 ....47 C3
Yorkshire Air Mus★
YO41 ....30 A1
Yorkshire Mus of Farming★
YO19 ....22 B4
Yorkshire Mus★ YO30 .64 A3
York Sixth Form Coll
................60 A3
York Sta YO24 ....65 A2
York St ⑤ YO19 .....23 A1
York Steiner Sch YO10 56 C1

List of numbered locations

In some busy areas of the maps it is not always possible to show the name of every place.

Where not all names will fit, some smaller places are shown by a number. If you wish to find out the name associated with a number, use this listing.

The places in this list are also listed normally in the Index.

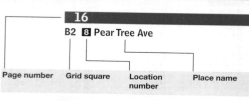

16
B2 ⑧ Pear Tree Ave

Page number   Grid square   Location number   Place name

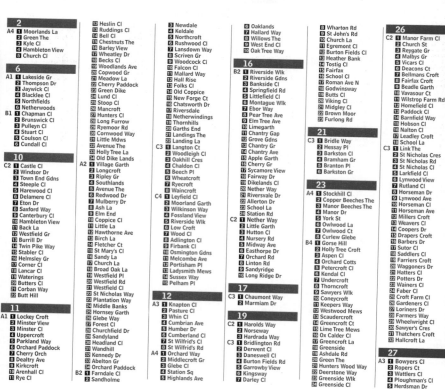

2
A4 ① Moorlands La
② Green The
③ Kyle Cl
④ Hambleton View
⑤ Church Cl

6
A1 ① Lakeside Gr
② Thompson Dr
③ Jaywick Cl
④ Blacklee Cl
⑤ Northfields
⑥ Netherwoods
B1 ① Chapman Cl
② Brunswick Cl
③ Pulleyn Cl
④ Stuart Cl
⑤ Coulson Cl
⑥ Cundall Cl

10
C2 ① Castle Cl
② Windsor Dr
③ Town End Gdns
④ Steeple Cl
⑤ Harewood Cl
⑥ Delamere Cl
⑦ Eton Dr
⑧ Saxford Way
⑨ Canterbury Cl
⑩ Hambleton View
⑪ Back La
⑫ Westfield Cl
⑬ Burrill Dr
⑭ Twin Pike Way
⑮ Stabler Cl
⑯ Helmsley Gr
⑰ Corner Cl
⑱ Lancar Cl
⑲ Waterings
⑳ Butters Cl
㉑ Corban Way
㉒ Butt Hill

11
A1 ① Lockey Croft
② Minster View
③ Minster Cl
④ Uppercroft
⑤ Parkland Way
⑥ Orchard Paddock
⑦ Cherry Orch
⑧ Dealtry Ave
⑨ Kirkcroft
⑩ Arenhall Cl
⑪ Rye Cl

⑫ Heslin Cl
⑬ Ruddings Cl
⑭ Bell Cl
⑮ Chestnuts The
⑯ Barley View
⑰ Wheatley Dr
⑱ Becks Cl
⑲ Woodlands Ave
⑳ Copwood Gr
㉑ Meadow La
㉒ Cherry Paddock
㉓ Green Dike
㉔ Lund Cl
㉕ Stoop Cl
㉖ Mancroft
㉗ Hunters Cl
㉘ Long Furrow
㉙ Ryemoor Rd
㉚ Cornwood Way
㉛ Little Mdws
㉜ Avenue The
㉝ Holly Tree La
㉞ Old Dike Lands
A2 ① Village Garth
② Longcroft
③ Ripley Gr
④ Southlands
⑤ Avenue The
⑥ Redwood Dr
⑦ Mulberry Dr
⑧ Ash La
⑨ Elm End
⑩ Coppice Cl
⑪ Little La
⑫ Hawthorne Ave
⑬ Birch La
⑭ Fletcher Ct
⑮ St Mary's Cl
⑯ Sandy La
⑰ Church La
⑱ Broad Oak La
⑲ Westfield Pl
⑳ Westfield Rd
㉑ Westfield Cl
㉒ St Nicholas Way
㉓ Plantation Way
㉔ Middle Banks
㉕ Hornsey Garth
㉖ Glebe Way
㉗ Forest Cl
㉘ Churchfield Dr
㉙ Sandyland
㉚ Headland Cl
㉛ Wandhill
㉜ Kennedy Dr
㉝ Abelton Gr
㉞ Orchard Paddock
B2 ① Farndale Cl
② Sandholme

③ Newdale
④ Keldale
⑤ Northcroft
⑥ Rushwood Cl
⑦ Lansdown Way
⑧ Scriven Gr
⑨ Woodcock Way
⑩ Falcon Cl
⑪ Mallard Way
⑫ Hall Rise
⑬ Folks Cl
⑭ Old Coppice
⑮ New Forge Cl
⑯ Chatsworth Dr
⑰ Riversdale
⑱ Netherwindings
⑲ Thornhills
⑳ Garths End
㉑ Landings The
㉒ Landing La
C3 ① Langton Ct
② Woodleigh Cl
③ Oakhill Cres
④ Chaldon Cl
⑤ Beech Pl
⑥ Wheatcroft
⑦ Ryecroft
C4 ① Leyfield Cl
② Moorland Garth
③ Wilkinson Way
④ Fossland View
⑤ Riverside Wlk
⑥ Low Croft
⑦ Wood Cl
⑧ Adlington Cl
⑨ Firbank Cl
⑩ Osmington Gdns
⑪ Melcombe Ave
⑫ Ladysmith Mews
⑬ Sussex Way
⑭ Pelham Pl

12
A3 ① Knapton Cl
② Pasture Cl
③ Whin Cl
④ Cumbrian Ave
⑤ Humber Dr
⑥ Cumberland Cl
⑦ St Wilfrid's Cl
⑧ St Wilfrid's Rd
A4 ① Orchard Way
② Middlecroft Dr
③ Glebe Cl
④ Station Sq
⑤ Highlands Ave

⑥ Oaklands
⑦ Hallard Way
⑧ Willows The
⑨ West End Cl
⑩ Oak Tree Way

16
B2 ① Riverside Wlk
② Riverside Gdns
③ Bankside Cl
④ Springfield Rd
⑤ Littlefield Cl
⑥ Montague Wlk
⑦ Ebor Way
⑧ Pear Tree Ave
⑨ Elm Tree Ave
⑩ Limegarth
⑪ Chantry Gap
⑫ Grove Gdns
⑬ Chantry Gr
⑭ Chantry Ave
⑮ Apple Garth
⑯ Cherry Gr
⑰ Sycamore View
⑱ Dikelands Cl
⑲ Nether Way
⑳ Riversvale Dr
㉑ Allerton Dr
㉒ School La
㉓ Station Rd
C2 ① Nether Way
② Little Garth
③ Hutton Cl
④ Nursery Rd
⑤ Midway Ave
⑥ Easthorpe Dr
⑦ Orchard Rd
⑧ Linton Rd
⑨ Sandyridge
⑩ Long Ridge Dr

17
C3 ① Chaumont Way
② Marmiam Dr

19
C2 ① Harolds Way
② Norseway
③ Hardrada Way
C3 ① Bridlington Rd
② Derwent Cl
③ Daneswell Cl
④ Burton Fields Rd
⑤ Garrowby View
⑥ Kingsway
⑦ Darley Cl

⑧ Wharton Rd
⑨ St John's Rd
⑩ Church La
⑪ Egremont Cl
⑫ Burton Fields Cl
⑬ Heather Bank
⑭ Fairfax
⑮ Tostig Cl
⑯ School Cl
⑰ Roman Ave N
⑱ Godwinsway
⑲ Butts Cl
⑳ Viking Cl
㉑ Midgley Cl
㉒ Brown Moor
㉓ Furlong Rd

21
C3 ① Bridle Way
② Hessay Pl
③ Barkston Cl
④ Bramham Gr
⑤ Branton Pl
⑥ Barkston Gr

23
A4 ① Stockhill Cl
② Copper Beeches The
③ Manor Beeches The
④ Manor Dr
⑤ York St
⑥ Owlwood La
⑦ Owlwood Ct
⑧ Curlew Glebe
B4 ① Gorse Hill
② Holly Tree Croft
③ Aspen Cl
④ Orchard Cotts
⑤ Petercroft Cl
⑥ Kendal Cl
⑦ Undercroft
⑧ Thorncroft
⑨ Sawyers Wlk
⑩ Coneycroft
⑪ Keepers Way
⑫ Westwood Mews
⑬ Scaudercroft
⑭ Lime Tree Mews
⑮ Ox Calder Cl
⑯ Greencroft La
⑰ Greenside
⑱ Ashdale Rd
⑲ Green The
⑳ Hunters Wood Way
㉑ Deerstone Way
㉒ Greenside Wlk
㉓ Greenside Cl

26
C2 ① Manor Farm Cl
② Church St
③ Reygate Gr
④ Malbys Gr
⑤ Vicars Cl
⑥ Deacons Ct
⑦ Bellmans Croft
⑧ Fairfax Croft
⑨ Beadle Garth
⑩ Vavasour Ct
⑪ Wilstrop Farm Rd
⑫ Homefield Cl
⑬ Paddock Cl
⑭ Barnfield Way
⑮ Hobson Cl
⑯ Nalton Cl
⑰ Leadley Croft
⑱ School La
C3 ① Link The
② St Nicholas Cres
③ St Nicholas Gr
④ St Nicholas Cl
⑤ Larkfield Cl
⑥ Lynwood View
⑦ Rutland Cl
⑧ Horseman Dr
⑨ Lynwood Ave
⑩ Horseman Cl
⑪ Horseman Ave
⑫ Millers Croft
⑬ Weavers Cl
⑭ Coopers Dr
⑮ Drapers Croft
⑯ Barbers Dr
⑰ Sutor Cl
⑱ Saddlers Cl
⑲ Farriers Croft
⑳ Waggoners Dr
㉑ Hatters Cl
㉒ Potters Dr
㉓ Wainers Cl
㉔ Faber Cl
㉕ Croft Farm Cl
㉖ Gardeners Cl
㉗ Loriners Dr
㉘ Farmers Way
㉙ Wheelwright Cl
㉚ Sawyer's Cres
㉛ Thatchers Croft
㉜ Hallcroft La

27
A3 ① Bowyers Cl
② Ropers Ct
③ Wattlers Cl
④ Ploughman's Cl
⑤ Herdsman Dr

Bus routes in and around York

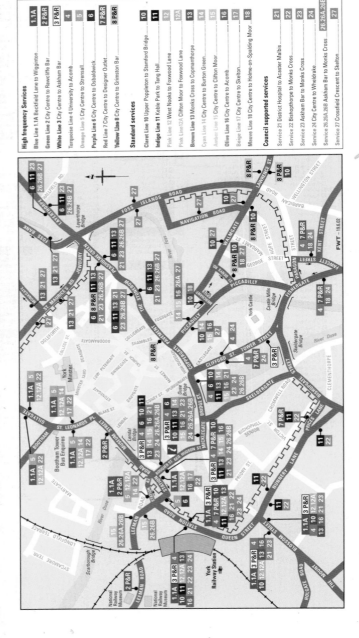

High frequency Services

- **1, 1A** Blue Line 1,1A Beckfield Lane to Wigginton
- **2 P&R** Green Line 2 City Centre to Rawcliffe Bar
- **3 P&R** White Line 3 City Centre to Askham Bar
- **4** Turquoise Line 4 University to Acomb
- **5** Orange Line 5 City Centre to Strensall
- **6** Purple Line 6 City Centre to Osbaldwick
- **7 P&R** Red Line 7 City Centre to Designer Outlet
- **8 P&R** Yellow Line 8 City Centre to Grimston Bar

Standard services

- **10** Claret Line 10 Upper Poppleton to Stamford Bridge
- **11** Indigo Line 11 Keble Park to Tang Hall
- **12** Pink Line 12 West Nooks to Foxwood Lane
- **12A** Pink Line 12A Clifton Moor to Foxwood Lane
- **13** Brown Line 13 Monks Cross to Copmanthorpe
- **14** Cyan Line 14 City Centre to Burton Green
- **15** Amber Line 15 City Centre to Clifton Moor
- **16** Olive Line 16 City Centre to Skelton
- **17** Beige Line 17 City Centre to Acomb
- **18** Mauve Line 18 City Centre to Holme-on-Spalding Moor

Council supported services

- **21** Service 21 District Hospital to Acaster Malbis
- **22** Service 22 Bishopthorpe to Monks Cross
- **23** Service 23 Askham Bar to Monks Cross
- **24** Service 24 City Centre to Wheldrake
- **26, 26A, 26B** Service 26,26A,26B Askham Bar to Monks Cross
- **27** Service 27 Crossfield Crescent to Skelton